How to Write Action/Adventure Novels

About the Author

Mike Newton has had an active life. Author of more than 80 books written over an eleven-year period, he has taught junior high school and worked as a security guard for the family of country-western singer Merle Haggard. Newton's work includes nonfiction (primarily "true crime"), westerns, and over four dozen action/adventure novels. His wife, Judy, is also an author with three books completed and three more in the works. The frighteningly prolific Newton family lives in Nashville, Indiana.

HOW TO WRITE
ACTION
ADVENTURE
NOVELS

by
Michael Newton

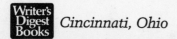 Cincinnati, Ohio

93 92 91 90 89   5 4 3 2 1

**Library of Congress Cataloging in Publica-
tion Data**

Newton, Michael
    How to write action/adventure novels/by
Michael Newton.
        p. cm.
    Includes index.
    ISBN 0-89879-358-0
    1. Adventure stories—Authorship. I. Title
PN3377.5.A37N48 1989   89-5546
808.3′87—dc 19   CIP

Designed by Carol Buchanan

The following two pages constitute an exten-
sion of this copyright page.

Permissions

For **Don** *and* **Mack,** *without whom.* . . .

"The great end of life is not knowledge but action."

Thomas Henry Huxley

"I myself must mix with action, lest I wither by despair."

Alfred, Lord Tennyson

"Life is either a daring adventure or nothing."

Helen Keller

"As life is action and passion, it is required of man that he should share the passion and action of his time, at peril of being judged not to have lived."

Oliver Wendell Holmes, Jr.

"It is only in adventure that some people succeed in knowing themselves—in finding themselves."

André Gide

Contents

1. Adventure Writers— Born or Made?

I became a novelist by accident.

Impossible, you say? Not quite.

I grew up in a family that encouraged reading, and I'd always been a bookworm, though my taste in literature admittedly diverged from what my parents might have wished. We lived close by a liquor store that featured paperbacks and magazines, and by the time I got to elementary school I was already nurturing a fondness-cum-obsession for "men's magazines"—the pulp variety, distinguished from the "nudies" by their covers, which depicted men of action locked in combat with assorted tigers, jaguars, pythons, and the scowling enemies of sundry foreign wars. My parents were concerned, to say the least, until my teacher (bless her!) offered up some sage advice. In essence, she suggested that my family might as well allow me to pursue my interests openly, instead of forcing me to go behind their backs and read the latest blood-and-guts extravaganza on the sly.

The rest, as someone said, is history.

The men's adventure magazines, I'm sorry to report, have long since disappeared, but in due time I made the shift to full-length books—adventure, Westerns, horror, war or crime—and I discovered that I liked to write as well as read. I found real pleasure in the research papers that made other students cringe in school, and on occasion I suspected I might like to "try a book" someday. Not *now*, of course . . . but *someday*.

In the early 1970s, two publishing events conspired to sneak up on my blind side and make "someday" a reality. A rash of fictional biographies were published, dealing with the lives of favorite characters from series fiction—Sherlock Holmes, James Bond, Doc Savage, Tarzan—and Don

Pendleton, a former-aerospace-technician-turned-adventure-writer, gave birth to the genre currently described by friend and foe alike as "action/adventure."

I had followed Pendleton's creation, "Executioner" Mack Bolan, through some twenty-five adventures when it suddenly occurred to me that he — the character, that is — deserved a separate and distinct biography, outside the series proper. Who should write it? Who, indeed!

Undaunted by the fact that I had published nothing, other than a few bizarre and ill-considered letters to the editor, I fired a query off to Pinnacle Books, then publishers of the Executioner series, putting my suggestion on the record. Time went by, and whimsy being what it is, I had forgotten all about the letter some months later, when I was astounded to receive a call from Pendleton himself. My query had laboriously made its way "through channels" to his desk, and while he wasn't overly excited by my premise, he was working on a concept that was vaguely similar. There might be room for a collaborator in the deal, if I could send along some clippings of my published work.

Blind panic. *Published work?* The kind that people *read?*

Incredibly, Don didn't laugh or slam the phone down when he learned that he was talking to a hapless would-be writer. He consented to review some articles which had been gleefully rejected by a string of editors, and he liked my style enough to grant me an audition for his latest project. The result was publication of my first successful work, as well as an apprenticeship of sorts, which taught me more about my chosen craft than any writing class could possibly convey.

My maiden voyage into print consisted of a chapter in *The Executioner's War Book* (Pinnacle, 1977). Eleven years and seventy-nine books later, I've seen Mack through twenty-four adventures on my own (out of 117 episodes released to date), and my installments in the series have sold more than three million copies since 1982.

The moral? Action/adventure writers are made, not born.

I came to writing and the Pendleton apprenticeship much like a student going off to trade school. Fiction was a "phase" that I would pass through, I supposed, en route to the creation of sensational and "relevant" nonfiction work. My target of the moment was the King assassination, which I planned to "crack" in print, thereby achieving fame and wealth while simultaneously pulling off a major public service. The completed manuscript weighed in at something like 900 pages, and it racked up twenty-odd rejections in the next three years; in 1980, slashed to one-third of its original length, it sold to an obscure paperback house and promptly sank without a ripple in the market. Meanwhile, waiting for the "big break" to arrive, I had already sold a dozen novels and a children's book.

In short, goals change. The difference between a would-be writer and a working author is *the sale*.

I still have dreams about nonfiction, and I try to keep my hand in with assorted reference volumes, but the hard fact is that ninety percent of my sales have been fiction, and most of those fall in the genre of action/adventure. I like it there, and I no longer feel the need to "rise above" the genre, searching for some "higher plane."

There's nothing new about the kind of snobbery that looks on genre writing with disdain. Forget about reviews of anything so "common" as adventure fiction; many critics won't admit that paperbacks *exist*, much less that anything of value may be found between their covers. I won't speculate on whether literary critics are, in fact, frustrated would-be authors, though there seems to be some evidence supporting that conclusion. (Roger Ebert, in the realm of cinematic criticism, is renowned for caustic jibes at actors and directors, but he seldom makes a reference to his own career in movie-making. Ebert's bomb, *Beyond the Valley of the Dolls*, is usually ranked among the most sadistic, sexist, generally repugnant exploitation films in living memory. And what about Rex Reed, in *Myra Breckenridge?*) For the record, let's just say there aren't a lot of literary critics with their names on novels currently in print.

A friend and fellow action writer, William Fieldhouse, once described for me his meeting with an individual who asked him when he planned to write "something serious." Bill's answer, which I cherish, was that *everything* he writes is serious. It's how he makes his living, after all, and he would soon be out of business if he went to work each day with attitudes of what-the-hell.

My favorite close encounter of the snobbish kind took place in grad school. I had signed up for a literary criticism course (what else?), and wound up sitting next to an acquaintance I had worked with years ago, behind the grill at Golden Arches. As we brought each other up to date, I learned my friend was "into" poetry; in fact, he had been paying magazines to print his verse. I told him I was writing action novels for an L.A. pub-

3

lisher and pulling in four hundred bucks per manuscript. (It sounds like chicken feed today, but at the time, 150 pages covered two months' rent.) When I suggested that he might try something similar, the poet smiled and hit me with a classic line: "I'll think about it, if I ever want to prostitute my art."

Okay.

We parted friends. By that time in my relatively young career, I *knew* that he was wrong. You can't sell out unless you give a project less than all you've got.

It doesn't faze me anymore—at least, not much—when critics, Ivy League professors, or psychologists take quill in hand to dump on "popular fiction." The day my books *aren't* popular, I'll start to worry. In the meantime, I'm too busy telling stories.

That's the nice thing about writing action/adventure. Readers by the millions realize what literary critics and professors often fail to grasp: the fact that genre writing isn't necessarily inferior. It is a discipline—an art form—that demands the very best a writer has to offer.

I suppose it boils down to a question of respect.

A writer who does not respect his audience (remember them? the people you expect to shell out hard-earned money for the pleasure of your company?) cannot expect the readers to keep coming back for more. A writer who does not respect himself, or his material, is wasting everybody's time.

If you approach your subject matter—genre fiction, mainstream, or whatever—with a clothespin on your nose, you can expect your readers to respond in kind. They may forgive a shaky subplot, undernourished characters, or faulty grammar, but a rip-off by a condescending "artist" is a bitter pill to swallow, and you won't find many folks out there who ask for seconds. Every writer, first and foremost, is a storyteller who has an obligation to present his chosen subject matter in the best, most entertaining form available.

If you're still with me, chances are you already possess the first prerequisite for action writing—namely, an attraction for the genre. Fascination isn't half the battle, but it *is* a long step forward. In the coming chapters, we'll examine genre history and learn to read the modern market; we'll discover how an action novel comes together, from the germ of an idea to final copy; we'll discuss the finer points of plotting, creating dialogue, and bringing characters to life, while coping with the "problems" raised by sex and violence in adventure fiction. Manuscript mechanics and the details of submission are included, with an eye toward eliminating the roadblocks to potential sales.

The action genre is a relatively new publishing industry which has ample room for authors who approach their subject with a sense of style. Before we find out where the market's going, though, we need to take a look at where it's been, the origins of action writing as a medium distinct and separate from its peers. For that, we need to visit Pittsfield, Massachusetts, on a summer afternoon in 1969.

2. A World of High (and Not-So-High) Adventure

My recon is complete and target identification is positive. Laurenti is the wheel, the OIC of the local setup. Every night at 1750 hours his car is parked at the curb in front by the man called Mister Erwin. The other Mister is a troop called Janus—Mister Janus. Must be some kind of a joke. The only ones they call "Mister" are the ones with side-arms. The one who looks like a salesman is named Brokaw. The college-boy type is Pete Rodriguez. The five of them leave the office at 1800 hours every night, and go out to their substations to pick up collections from their legmen. Later they make personal calls on slow accounts. But not tomorrow night! The Executioner has a little collection substation of his own all set up, on the fourth floor of the Delsey building. It's a perfect drop. I ran my triangulations last night and again tonight. It will be like picking rats out of a barrel. The targets will not have anyplace to go but down—to the ground. I timed out at six seconds on the dry run tonight and that was figuring them to scatter in all directions after the first round. I think I will better that time tomorrow because I do not believe these troops have been under fire before. I will probably be half done before the reaction even begins. Well, we will see.

With that pronouncement, "Executioner" Mack Bolan launched his *War Against the Mafia* and introduced a new dimension to the field of action novels. Nineteen years beyond that first barrage in Pittsfield, he is going strong with 117 episodes in print and no end in sight.

In Chapter 1, I called Don Pendleton the father of the action genre. It is probably more accurate to label Don a pioneer, blazing the trail for a new generation of writers to follow. In the early days, his novels were the spearhead of a revolution in adventure fiction, but it took a while for Don to realize precisely what he'd done.

A New World of Adventure

The revolution actually began with Bee Line Books, a porno house that sought to go legit in 1969 by altering its name to Pinnacle and grinding out a crop of action thrillers. One of those was Pendleton's unique and energetic story of a Green Beret recalled from Asian duty to arrange the funerals of his parents and his sister. Driven to the brink of madness by harassment from a team of loan sharks, Bolan's father shot the other members of the family before he turned his weapon on himself. Untouchable through legal means, the local mafiosi were expected to escape scot-free, until a grim avenger took their case in hand, annihilating those responsible for shattering his family, moving on to spread a reign of terror throughout the local syndicate.

Originally titled *Duty Killer*, altered to *The Executioner* by press time, Bolan's saga took the industry by storm; it also took Don Pendleton and Pinnacle completely by surprise. *The Executioner*'s phenomenal success led to eight hot sequels in the next two years and encouraged Pinnacle to follow up with other heroes bearing lethal monikers — *The Penetrator*, *The Destroyer*, *The Death Merchant*, *The Butcher*, *The Vigilante* — emerging as the hottest series house in business.

Stung by Pinnacle's success, competitors weighed in with copycats like *Killinger*, *The Marksman*, *The Assassin*, *The Survivalist*, *The Mercenary*. Even old Nick Carter, hero of a series that preceded Bolan's 1969 debut, received a face-lift from his editors, emerging as the *Kill Master*.

The new crop of heroes did not spring full-grown from thin air. While their weapons were new, their targets ripped from tomorrow's headlines, they maintained a historic tradition of adventure fiction dating back to *Beowulf*. Classic works like *Kidnapped*, *Treasure Island*, and *Swiss Family Robinson* continued the line in later generations, while Jules Verne added a dash of science fiction to his action yarns like *Journey to the Center of the Earth*. The exploits of Tarzan, Doc Savage, and Conan are patently action/adventure, following the evolution of "the pulps," which later fueled my own imagination as a child. Beginning in 1953, James Bond carried the ball with continental flair, racking up some impressive body-counts against SPECTER, SMERSH, and the Spangled Mob.

In short, adventure's been around forever, but its face has changed.

Unlike the heroes who had gone before, protagonists of modern action novels were required to cope with Evil on its own malignant terms. No cavalry was galloping to save the day, and readers of the genre seemed to understand that good guys finish last unless they finish off the bad guys first. The righteous loner with a heart of gold and fists of steel could never hope to stand against the Mafia or KGB. He needed Uzis, rocket launchers, M-16s.

The newborn genre's startling success emerged from many factors, one of which must be conceded as a pure coincidence of timing, vis-à-vis contemporary world events. In Vietnam, America's self-confidence was shattered by the Tet offensive, and the grunts dug in for four long years of brutal combat by attrition. On the home front, angry demonstrations, urban riots, and a rising tide of street crime strained the fabric of society, the rifts exacerbated by judicial rulings that appeared to favor criminals. New exposés of syndicated crime, as typified by *The Valachi Papers*, taught Americans about the nation's "hidden government."

Within this atmosphere, the action genre's central theme—dynamic hero figures taking on the heavies with assistance from the latest military hardware—struck responsive chords among a generation weaned on "anti-heroes," as personified by grubby outlaws in *The Wild Bunch*, unwashed vagabonds in *Easy Rider*, sleazy "lawmen" in *The French Connection*. Action novels—and their cinematic counterparts in films like *Dirty Harry*—offered clean, vicarious solutions to frustration, anger, fear. Along the way, their authors also did a bang-up job of entertaining millions . . . which, as we've established, is the basic task of any storyteller.

The latter 1970s observed a brief decline in action series; of the early crush, no more than three or four survived. Their swift demise was brought on by recession and American withdrawal from the war in Vietnam, cessation of the "long hot summers," and the advent of a new Me Generation. The Mafia was still around, but marathon publicity had robbed it of its novelty, its menace. There were even wistful indications that the New York mob families, running short of members, were forced to import greenhorns from impoverished villages in Sicily. The "gang that couldn't shoot straight" was a public laughingstock.

Times change, however, and within a few short years, action/adventure got a new shot in the arm from rampant terrorism, hostage crises, and the ineffectual response to same by home-grown statesmen. Heroes were again in short supply, and therefore in demand. Before the 1980s had a chance to gather steam, another pack of macho men were off and running, and a few dynamic heroines had been created who were prepared to match their stride. And, with some minor variations wrought by time, those new arrivals constitute the action market as it stands today.

The Marketplace

The modern action genre now includes a number of important subdivisions that beginning writers should consider as potential points of entry to the marketplace. The *paramilitary hero* has remained a staple of the genre, with Mack Bolan and his fellow pioneers encountering stiff competition from the likes of *Hawker*, *The Specialist*, the *SOBs*, and *Cody's Army*, just to name a few. Since carrying his war from Pinnacle to Gold Eagle Books, the Executioner has taken a cue from television, giving rise to spin-off series in the form of *Able Team* and *Phoenix Force*. (Ironically, while Rambo has emerged for many fans as the penultimate adventure hero, he was actually killed off in the novel *First Blood*, revived in the published sequels through some editorial sleight-of-hand.) In tune with modern headlines, heroes of the action genre now apply themselves to terrorists and street gangs, killer cults and neo-fascists, in addition to the proven heavies of the mob and Moscow.

Men at war have captured a substantial section of the market during recent years. The series set in World War II (*The Sergeant*, *The Rat Bastards*) have experienced a poor response from action readers, in comparison to tales of Vietnam. New series like *The Gunships*, *Vietnam: Ground Zero*, *The Black Eagles*, *Chopper 1*, and others give Americans a second chance to do it right in Southeast Asia. History may be inviolate in terms of winners and losers, but the action genre paints a rather different portrait of the veterans who were reviled at home as "baby-killers."

In the early 1970s, a rash of *martial arts* adventure series swept the market, cashing in on the success of Bruce Lee's films and David Carradine's television series, *Kung Fu*. Some of them can still be found in used-book stores, their cover art resembling Chinese movie posters, boasting titles like *Karate Killers* and *Kung Fu Avenger*. Some showed real imagination, like the Western series *Six-Gun Samurai*, but as Chuck Norris has been forced to try for movies with at least the vestige of a plot behind the snap-kicks, so the various karate series faded in the stretch. Of the original contestants, only *The Destroyer* has survived, and it was never solely martial arts from the beginning. Recent efforts — *Chant*, from Berkley-Jove, for instance — have a minor following, but nothing would-be authors can afford to stake their hopes on.

Mel Gibson's box office bonanza in *The Road Warrior* produced a rash of postapocalyptic action novels, facing rugged heroes off against the perils of America laid waste. A few, like *The Survivalist* and *Doomsday Warrior*, wage unending war against the Russian occupying army. Most — like *Deathlands*, *Endworld*, *Phoenix*, and *The Traveler* — are set against the backdrop of a new Stone Age, complete with mutant life forms and a drastically revised geography. (The postapocalyptic theme has even taken root in juvenile fiction with series like *Firebrats* and *After the Bomb*, which tone down sex and violence to suit their more delicate readers.)

A fairly recent entry to the action field has been embodied in the trend toward *techno-thrillers*. Clive Cussler, author of *Firefox* and *Raise the Titanic*, is a groundbreaker in this area. Another winner in the techno-thriller sweepstakes is Tom Clancy, who presents his readers with state-of-the-art weaponry and surveillance equipment in *Patriot Games*, *Red Storm Rising*, and *The Hunt for Red October*. Fans of techno-thrillers want their gadgetry authentic (or, at least, authentic-sounding), and they thrive on novels like *Kill the Potemkin*, *Flight of the Old Dog*, and *The Fifth Horseman*. Research may be called for on the part of authors who are not mechanically inclined, but if you've always had a secret yen to be an engineer — or if you *are* an engineer! — this field may be for you.

Another subdivision of the action genre, borrowing substantially from a related discipline, consists of the new *"adult" Westerns*. Pioneered, ironically, by Briton George G. Gilman in the 1960s, with his *Edge* and *Steele* series from Pinnacle, adult Westerns differ from their traditional ancestors in the same way adult films deviate from family fare, namely, in amounts of sex and violence. In series such as *Longarm*, *The Gunsmith*, *The Scout*, and *The Trailsman*, our heroes get lucky with women as often as six-guns or cards. This subject area is also one where lusty heroines have proven their ability to grapple with the guys in offerings like *Lone Star*, *Buckskin*, *The White Squaw*, and *Arizona Hellcat*. Generally speaking, Westerns are an area where books *can* be evaluated by their covers; look for blood and lots of cleavage on the new adult variety, reflecting content with a fair degree of accuracy. Traditional oaters are more sedate, inside and out, devoting more attention to development of characters and settings, as a general rule of thumb.

Westerns aren't the only genre that has made at least a partial crossover into action/adventure, though the other hybrids have enjoyed a mixed reception in the marketplace. *Police procedurals* have overlapped with short-lived series like *The Hunter*, *Sledge*, and *Dirty Harry*, but their popularity has faded in the stretch and none remain in print today. You'll generally find the action novels shelved with *mysteries* in major chain stores, but they really don't belong there. In the hard-core action genre, there is seldom any lasting doubt about "whodunnit." Rather, we are served our villains early on, with relish, and the story marches toward their ultimate comeuppance in a blaze of gunfire. Any twists and turns along the way are icing on the cake.

Some tales of fantasy, especially the *sword and sorcery* variety, appear to have as much in common with the action genre as they do with fairy tales or science fiction. One or two, like *Raven*, have been lately billed by publishers as "action-fantasy," and fans of Conan the Barbarian, Doc Savage, even Tarzan, have been sampling some pretty hard-core action since the 1920s. If there is a clear dividing line between the modern action novels and this venerable subdivision, we shall find it in *reality*. The modern action hero pits himself against a panoply of real-life monsters — mafiosi, terrorists, and psychopathic killers — in familiar (if exotic) settings. There is no resort to spells or magic swords, no surgery (*à la* Doc Savage) that can change the heavies into choir boys overnight.

Occult adventures got off to a rocky start in 1970, with Michael Avalone's *Satan Sleuth*, but found a more receptive audience in Europe, whence *The Night Hunter*, a British import, has arrived to test domestic markets. *Movie tie-ins* have been more successful; readers have seen box-office gold trickle down to the bookstores on novelizations of screenplays for *Rambo*, *Predator*, *The Terminator*, *Magnum Force*, *Invasion USA*, and *The Exterminator*.

While we're talking feature films, it should be noted that modern action/adventure novels have a poor track record for translation to the silver screen. With the notable exception of *First Blood* (which spun off to the

Rambo series), no major action novel has been able to take Hollywood by storm. *The Executioner, The Warlord, The Survivalist,* and other series have been optioned off to major studios for years—in Bolan's case, for decades—but with passing time, the chances of their actual production grow increasingly remote. It took *The Destroyer* fifteen years to turn up on film, and the result—a classic dud called *Remo Williams*—self-destructed at the box office, going down with all hands in a sea of red ink, to a chorus of well-deserved hoots from the critics.

New writers with movies in mind may have better results with an original screenplay—provided they also have talent, mechanical skills, and the requisite discipline, plus a few contacts in Tinsel Town. (More on submission techniques in an upcoming chapter.) A glance at the theater listings, a stroll through your neighborhood video outlet, and *voilà*!, you'll turn up adventure aplenty. While films like *Commando, Raw Deal, Lethal Weapon,* and *Cobra* may not figure high in the race for an Oscar, they're all making money . . . and so are their writers. The recent profusion of action/adventure on film (and TV, to a lesser extent) offers new genre writers one more avenue of attack.

The Audience

Obviously, there's a ready market for the kind of rugged action heroes typified by Bolan, Rambo, Remo Williams, and their breed. But who, precisely, are the readers?

Based upon a demographic study executed by Gold Eagle Books in 1985, it would appear that roughly 85 percent of them are male. Approximately half of those are under thirty-five years old, and a substantial number are (or have been) military personnel or law enforcement officers. They share a more-or-less pervasive interest in weapons, martial arts, and paramilitary tactics as applied to vigorous suppression of "the bad guys."

Raw statistics, though, present a hollow, fragmentary portrait of the "average" action reader. For a more complete appraisal, we must listen to those readers, one-on-one. A sampling of fan mail generated by Gold Eagle's buyers, provided courtesy of the publisher's reader-management editor, displays the range of backgrounds, interests, and styles of action loyalists.

A high school student from Vancouver, Washington, explains: "The reason I keep reading your books is because before the eighth grade I never

13

really liked reading. In fact, I hated it with a passion. For school book reports, I checked out books but just made them up. I was finally introduced to your series by a friend, and halfway through the book I knew I wouldn't be making up any more reports. My book report grades have increased incredibly."

A lawyer from an East St. Louis suburb says: "I am writing as a long-time fan of yours who has collected every book in the series. I find them very enjoyable, and have passed them on to my sons, who also enjoy them."

From an army private: "I'm the sort of reader who likes a variety of literature. One night I could be engrossed in a novel by Steinbeck, Tolkien, or Stephen King, and the following evening totally enjoying one of your masterpieces."

A Florida teenager offers: "I'm writing to let you know I really enjoy reading your books. They are fast-paced and full of action. In my opinion, [the Executioner] represents what America should have at this time against terrorism. At times I wish I was Mack Bolan, defending the rights and beliefs of civilized men and women."

Another serviceman continues: "I was introduced to your series by a friend in high school. I am now twenty-two years old, serving in the U.S. Air Force, stationed in Japan. I enlisted in the military to fight for the ideals and beliefs that Mack Bolan has strived to protect."

And, finally, an ex-policeman writes: "I had to retire after twenty-six years with the police department due to a back injury and a gunshot wound which shattered my ankle bone. Being only forty-nine at the time of retirement, [the Bolan] series has helped me adjust. I have a complete set of your books, and have read the series five times."

In short, the action market is composed of men and women representing every walk of life, all ages. The abiding trait they share in common is a passion for adventure, whether it be set against the backdrop of a Third World battleground, an urban jungle, or the withered hellscape of a futuristic no-man's land.

Successful action writers serve as travel agents, carrying their readers far away from daily drudgery of creditors and housework, granting them an opportunity to cast routine aside and gamble with their lives, secure in the understanding that it's all a game. If you provide *your* readers with a memorable trip, they won't forget *you*, either. And a satisfying number will express their gratitude by picking up your next book, and the next. . . .

Before we start to count those dollar signs, however, let's explore the fundamentals that must be mastered on the road to high adventure. Every hero's quest must have a point of origin, and every story must begin with an idea.

3. For Openers . . .

What should I write about?

The classic question puzzles every writer—veterans as well as novices—at one time or another. Some will never get beyond it, bogging down in writer's block before they get a word on paper. Others write to hapless editors with the announcement that they're ready to begin their first big novel . . . if the editors will only furnish them with subject matter, plot, and characters. A few jump in feet-first, and manage to complete the job by pure, dumb luck.

I've often heard it said that "everybody has a book inside them." Hogwash. Many would-be writers don't possess the talent or imagination to produce a simple paragraph, much less a finished novel. Some who try (and fail) are great "idea men," capable of sketching brilliant thumbnail plots, but sadly lacking in the discipline required to see their projects through.

The authors who survive in genre fiction, or in mainstream, share a common dedication and determination to succeed. They aren't created equal—some may shine, while others barely glimmer—but they rise above the mass of "wanna-bees" through perseverance and at least a modicum of skill. No matter what their level of achievement, though, from "brand name" authors to their fledgling competition, all start out together, scrounging for the germ of an idea.

What should *you* write about?

Some authors may rely on inspiration for their hot ideas, but most, in modern action writing, seek a more substantial basis for their work. It's fine for Stephen King's protagonist in *Misery* to sit before his ancient Royal, waiting to "find the hole in the paper" and let his story "write itself," but

17

you can starve to death while waiting for a novel to appear by magic. Simply stated, folks, she just don't work that way.

Unless you're favored with a very lively muse, you'll need at least a general notion of your story as a launching pad, before you set to work. By "story," I'm referring to the *subject* of your novel, rather than the *plot*. As every freshman English student knows — or should know — *plot* consists of incidents that motivate assorted characters and move them on from the beginning of a story to its ultimate conclusion. *Subject*, on the other hand, refers to underlying themes, the basic "what" and "why" of any given tale, without which *plot* becomes a string of pointless and irrelevant scenarios.

You may not know precisely where your characters are going in a story, and you may decide to kill off some of your favorites before you're done, but if you don't know *what* they're trying to accomplish in the first place, you've got trouble on your hands.

So, where do stories come from?

Inspiration vs. Homework

Many authors draw on personal experience for inspiration, falling back upon the maxim that it's best to "write what you know." Ex-Green Beret Barry Sadler is a prime example; having first parlayed a tour of Vietnam into a million-selling record album, he now enjoys a successful career as a novelist in the action/adventure genre. Big-city police work has yielded several authors of note, including Robert Daley, Dorothy Uhnak, and Joseph Wambaugh. Service in the intelligence community provides a taste of gritty realism to novels written by E. Howard Hunt and Bill Fieldhouse, not to mention the late, great Ian Fleming.

The quest for raw experience is sometimes carried to extremes. One writer on the staff of *Able Team* (Gold Eagle Books) became so fascinated with the politics of Third World liberation struggles that he wound up in Sri Lanka, teaching martial arts to rebel forces, building barricades and booby traps while bloody riots raged around him in the streets. I generally would not recommend this type of "research" to the novice, but there's no denying that a taste of combat can provide new insight, bringing an immediacy to the printed page.

It isn't necessary for an author to be living on the edge, however, for experience to serve as inspiration. Even the most trivial, mundane event may offer grist for the creative mill. Stephen King's short story "Crouch

End" was inspired when King got lost in London's back streets, searching for a friend's address. In 1983, Gold Eagle's authors gathered for a two-day conference in Las Vegas, plotting new directions for their series. One of the attendees, Jerry Ahern, subsequently used the meeting as the centerpiece of an adventure novel. In *The Hard Way* (Gold Eagle, 1984), Ahern portrays a group of action writers, meeting in Las Vegas, who are taken hostage by a band of terrorists. They finally defeat the heavies, using weapons one of them habitually carries in his luggage, and the day is saved.

Assuming that you're not a mercenary, and you don't spend your vacations stalking terrorists or bugging embassies, you have another source of inspiration at your fingertips. That's right—the daily news! If you possess the requisite imagination to be writing novels in the first place, any network news show, any major urban daily should provide you with at least the germ of an idea. If you cannot rack up at least a dozen viable suggestions from the news in any given week, there's something badly out of whack. I'd recommend you try a different source, or take another look at the material in hand to jump-start your imagination.

Television and the movies fall back constantly on current issues as the basis for their action plots. In *Dirty Harry*, for example, the sadistic "Scorpio" is no more than a stand-in for a real-life killer, the elusive "Zodiac." (Unlike the heavy played by Andy Robinson, however, Zodiac is still at large.) A recent episode of TV's "Equalizer" squared the title hero off against an adult bully bent on harassing a small boy plagued with AIDS—a story lifted more or less intact from headlines out of Florida and Indiana. And if you're afflicted with insomnia some evening, don't waste time with sheep; try counting all the films and novels rooted in the controversy over MIAs in Vietnam.

I personally try to link my action novels with the latest news whenever possible. A blend of fact and fiction, if judiciously employed, adds authenticity—and it may entice new readers who are interested in your subject matter from their own perusal of the daily news. In 1981, when several members of the Ku Klux Klan were busted on the eve of their attempt to seize the island of Dominica, I saw potential for a story. Phasing out the Klan in favor of a neo-fascist billionaire with syndicate connections, planning an invasion of Grenada, I produced the novel *Paramilitary Plot* (Gold Eagle, 1982). Reports of Yakuza involvement in Las Vegas gambling inspired *The Bone Yard*, and a Sunday supplement on teenage runaways in

Southern California prompted me to write *Hollywood Hell* (both from Gold Eagle, 1985). In 1986, a "60 Minutes" segment dealing with Vietnamese "dust children" planted the seed for a revenge novel, *Child of Blood*, which sold to Bantam Books.

Sometimes, with luck, you get the jump on history. Six months before the flight crew of a skyjacked aircraft used their fire ax on a terrorist, with permanent results, I included a similar scene in the manuscript of *Flight 741* (Gold Eagle, 1986). And five full years before Islamic gunmen captured the *Achille Lauro*, I dispatched a team of Black September terrorists to seize the good ship *Crystal Belle*, in *Death Cruise* (Carousel, 1980).

Psychic? Hardly. Nor do I believe the PLO was studying my manuscript before they launched their raid. The fact is, if you learn enough about the real-life heavies, come to understand the way they think and operate, you may incorporate a realism in your work that offers a decided edge in making sales.

Avoiding Obsolescence

When shopping for a story line, beware of subjects bearing built-in deadlines, which may soon be obsolete. The novel you begin today will not be done tomorrow; it may not be done a year from now, and writing time is only one of several delays you must anticipate before your hot idea turns up in bookstores. Editing and publication of a novel both take time, and while a major house can grind out quickie paperbacks within two weeks, in cases of emergency, the average time is more like eighteen *months*, from your submission of a "finished" manuscript to its release through retail outlets. (The volume in your hands was purchased by its publisher in autumn 1987, for release in 1989.) It should be obvious that if you're sitting down in late November 1991, to start a novel based around the presidential race in '92, you've got potential timing problems on your hands.

This doesn't mean that "dated" novels are impossible to publish. Don Pendleton's *Canadian Crisis* (Pinnacle, 1975) placed Executioner Mack Bolan in the vicinity of Montreal's summer Olympics, and eight years later, *Balefire* sent a solitary Arab terrorist against the L.A. games. It happens, but in general, you'll find that editors prefer a theme that does not come complete with built-in obsolescence.

An obvious exception to the rule of thumb on dated themes involves historical events. John Jakes has made a fortune from the Civil War, and there is ample room within the action genre for incorporation of authentic history. Jack Higgins and Ken Follett are two masters of the craft, and now that Vietnam is history instead of prime-time news, a growing crop of authors are producing manuscripts about that war that range from the sublime to the ridiculous. At present, Vietnam is "hot" across the board — in literature, on television, at the movies — and the would-be writer looking for a point of entry to the action market could do worse than sailing up the Mekong for a one-on-one with Charlie.

Novels based on history would seem to have a clear advantage in the plot department; they can even call on real-life characters for cameo appearances, provided that the author knows his libel law. But woe to any writer who depends on history to tell a tale, relieving him or her of basic obligations as a storyteller. You are writing *fiction*, after all, and it is *not* enough to simply change some names, air-lift your characters to Bunker Hill or Gettysburg, and then proceed to plagiarize a college textbook for your story line. There is a world of difference between Del Vecchio's *The Thirteenth Valley* and a Time-Life volume on the war in Vietnam. Your readers count on you to amplify reality while providing solutions and, from time to time, a happy ending. If they wanted homework, they'd be taking classes at the local university instead of spending time with you.

Handling the Headlines

Precisely *how* are news reports converted into action novels? Once you get the hang of what to look for, what to ask yourself, it's not as tricky as it seems. I've randomly selected and synopsized ten news items, published in the week before I wrote this chapter. Names and the specific settings are deleted — they're irrelevant — and you should take a stab at spinning thumbnail story lines around each case before we tackle them together. Let's imagine that —

A. A free-lance American pilot is shot down and jailed in a hostile Third World country.
B. The U.N. opens up its files on Nazi war crimes . . . and 433 of them are missing.
C. The families of nine Americans killed in a foreign air crash complain the local government will not release any corpses for burial.

D. Soldiers of a Third World nation capture the reputed leader of a recent unsuccessful coup.
E. A fanatical Middle Eastern ruler announces creation of a "political will," naming his chosen successor.
F. Moments before a disastrous airplane crash, the pilot radios for help, reporting sounds of gunfire from the passenger compartment.
G. An unidentified woman, disguised as a nurse, kidnaps a newborn infant from a hospital maternity ward.
H. Soldiers on routine border patrol kill five foreign terrorists.
I. A chance misdemeanor arrest bags an international fugitive linked with terrorism, narcotics smuggling, and multiple murder.
J. A jealous husband shoots his wife, two children, and two neighbors, then commits suicide.

I grant you, these are easy, but they serve our purpose as examples. With imagination and a dash of background research, any one of the selected items should provide an adequate foundation—inspiration, if you will—for a respectable adventure novel. If you draw a blank on one or two, the other eight or nine should keep you busy for a while. If you strike out on *all* of them, relax; there'll be more news tomorrow, guaranteed.

For openers, I scan our sample clippings with a healthy dose of paranoia. Treachery, conspiracy, and good old-fashioned subterfuge are staples of the action genre. Wise adventure heroes trust themselves, their guns, and not much else. You're points ahead if you can make yourself familiar with the mind-set, taking on a front-line grunt's perspective as he scans the shadows for potential enemies.

In item A, I ask myself about the pilot, first of all. Is he a hero or a heavy? Was he actually breaking any laws, or is the hostile government just using him for leverage against America on some distinct and unrelated issue? If his actions *were* illegal, who's his sponsor? Who might wish to rescue him—or *silence* him—to salvage their illicit operation? Should a strike force be dispatched to liberate the hostage? And, if so, will other gunmen be en route to murder him before he can escape?

On item B, our crucial question is the contents of the missing files. Who stood to gain—or lose—by their convenient disappearance? Is some European statesman running for elective office, possibly concerned about disclosure of his Nazi past? Who has the files? Have they been stolen by the Nazis named therein? By an Israeli hit team? By some freelance thief who plans to offer them for sale to the highest bidder?

With item C, we face a multiplicity of questions that may launch us off into adventure land. Who were the nine Americans? What took them to the country where they died? Were any of them linked to the American intelligence community, "sensitive" industry, or organized crime? If they were simply tourists, what may one (or all) of them have seen that would have placed their lives in jeopardy? If your protagonist is sent to solve the mystery or bring specific bodies back, where should he start?

Coups and revolutions offer great potential for adventure writers. An example is *The Dogs of War*, by Frederick Forsyth, which pursues the toppling of a Third World government from its conception through the final firefight. In the case of item D, the capture of a revolutionary leader may be useful as the end — or the beginning — of your story. If the coup fails early on, survivors of the revolutionary force may try some other move against the government, perhaps enlisting mercenaries to support the cause. Your hero may fall out on either side, depending on your characterization of the ruling government, American interests in the area, and so forth.

Sudden instability in any oil-rich country is potentially explosive. Item E presents your hero(es) with a chance to alter history through any one of several means. Once they identify the loony tune's successor, will they seek to hinder or assist his rise to power? How, in either case, can this be best accomplished with the minimum amount of risk? Is this official business, or is someone in the private sector — a cartel of oil executives, for instance — picking up the tab?

In item F, the problem of the air crash is a sticky one. It may suggest a climax for your story, but I'm more inclined to have the "accident" up front, allowing the protagonist to search for answers and assess responsibility. If shots were fired inside the plane, who did the shooting? Why? Who were his targets? If you're "thinking paranoid," it should be obvious your hero won't just stumble on these answers free-of-charge. Behind the grim disaster there will certainly be *someone* seeking to suppress the truth at any cost . . . including future homicides.

On item G, the baby-napping is a different sort of problem. We are interested, of course, in the identity of the elusive "nurse," but first we have to scrutinize the victims. Are they government employees? Mobsters?

Millionaires? Participants in the protected-witness program? Once you have identified the baby's parents, you'll be well along your way toward motive and the ultimate identity of the kidnappers. Now, all you have to do is bring on a hero and get the child back! Simple, right?

A border incident like that described in item H is nothing new in Africa, the Middle East, or Central America. Your job is to *make* it new—and different—from any other showdown of its kind. Who were the terrorists, and what makes them unique? Was one of them an agent for the KGB? A hunted Nazi war criminal? An American agent recently listed as missing in action? Do they represent some new, virulent organization with evil plans in mind? And were they entering the country, or escaping *from* it, after making contact with allies on the inside?

With item I, we need to ask ourselves about the man in custody. Why does a high-class fugitive allow himself to be arrested in this kind of bargain-basement incident? Was his incarceration planned? If so, by whom? Is he more dangerous in jail than on the street? (Suppose the President is scheduled for a visit to the area, and your assassin is on hand, presumably secure in jail. . . .) Is the arrest a mere diversion on behalf of his associates, while they pull off the terrorist coup of the decade nearby?

The "loving father goes berserk" report in item J is all too common; two more have made headlines in the time between my clipping of the item and the writing of these lines. But keep in mind, we're "thinking paranoid" these days. *Is* this a murder-suicide, or something else entirely? Was the family wiped out, with Daddy framed (and killed) to take the fall? Who benefits from slaughtering a family—or were the *neighbors* actually targets of the triggerman? Again, who *were* the victims, really? Federal witnesses in hiding? Eastern bloc defectors? Relatives of a "retired" CIA agent? The possibilities are limited only by your own imagination.

If a headline grabs your fancy but you don't think it will make an adequate foundation for a novel, clip it anyway, for future reference. You never know when you may want a short vignette, digression, flashback, or whatever, to illuminate your story or your characters. The works of Joseph Wambaugh are replete with anecdotes about police work that appear to have no bearing on the plot, but they do wonders at providing atmosphere and bringing Wambaugh's characters to life. (The image of a black patrolman struggling to lynch a wino stands out in my mind as one of the high points in *The Glitter Dome*. I don't recall the plot in any detail, but that scene still comes to mind with regularity, and never fails to bring a smile.)

Nothing New Under the Sun?

Ideas cannot be copyrighted, but unless you're set on building up a reputation as a hack and rip-off artist, you will have to give some thought to that old bogeyman, *originality*. Make no mistake, developing original ideas can be a major problem. John Cawelti, in his survey of the modern Western, claims that there are only six clear themes in Western films or novels. Stephen King (who ought to know), asserts that horror stories may be slotted rather neatly into four thematic categories: vampires, werewolves, ghosts, and "things without a name."

I may be oversimplifying (and I'll certainly draw flack from authors who believe they've just devised the hottest concept for a story since the Book of Revelation), but I dare suggest that novels in the modern action genre all possess a single, common theme, which I will label *the heroic quest*. Within this concept, we have ample room for good and evil, treachery and righteous vengeance, good guys versus heavies. It doesn't matter if your hero(ine) is hunting MIAs or tackling a drug cartel, pursuing terrorists or tracking down a solitary maniac, the quest motif applies.

With that in mind, it should be no surprise that revolutionary new ideas for action plots are rare as hen's teeth. Of the series currently in print, only Barry Sadler's *Casca* comes to mind. Its hero is a Roman soldier, cursed by Jesus Christ on Calvary, condemned to live forever as a mercenary warrior in the dirtiest, most brutal wars of human history. If he gets killed in Vietnam, he pops up at the Little Big Horn. Now you see him, now you don't. It's interesting to note that Sadler had to dip his pen in fantasy to find a brand-new wrinkle for the action genre, and I'd say he's pulled it off in style.

The other end of the "creative" scale abounds in copycats and rip-offs, recently epitomized by *Firefight*, featuring a Rambo clone for cover art, a search for MIAs in Southeast Asia (sound familiar?), and a hero named— I kid you not—"Montana Jones"! Presumably, his cousin Indiana was away on other business when the SOS came through.

Most editors *do* notice rip-offs, by the way. Some years ago, a lazy would-be author mailed the outline of his "new" idea to editors at Gold Eagle Books, hoping for a spot on the *Executioner* writing team. There are these Russian sleeper agents in America, you see, all hypnotized to blot out memories of training by the Soviets, and now they're being triggered into suicidal acts of sabotage by phone calls from their KGB controller. It sounds promising . . . unless you've seen the movie *Telefon*, in which case you will recognize the "author's" outline as a flagrant act of piracy.

Great Minds with but a Single Thought

Between the two extremes of brilliant new ideas and outright plagiarism lies a world of tested, universal themes that may have life left in them yet. The challenge lies in working with a common theme, reshaping it, and making it your own. The fact that you decide to send your hero up against narcotics dealers doesn't mean you have to make him dress like Sonny Crockett on "Miami Vice" (or, God help us, like *The French Connection*'s Popeye Doyle).

Television and the movies hold all honors when it comes to the recycling of common themes. If you're a fan of situation comedies (and even if you're not), you have experienced what I refer to as the "I Love Lucy syndrome." Simply stated, "Lucyisms" are the story lines that got a laugh in 1952, and that return predictably, monotonously, turning up on every other show from "Mr. Ed" to "Mr. Belvedere." And while we're talking déjà vu, can anybody name a cop show where the hero's wife or girlfriend isn't killed or kidnapped once a season?

TV Guide, some years ago, published the tongue-in-cheek profile of a scriptwriter who was working his way through a copy of *Movies on TV*, recycling old plots and selling them—in alphabetical order, no less—to modern television producers. The piece was clearly meant as satire, but it still contained more truth than poetry—as witnessed by the Phantom of the Opera's recent guest appearance on "The Equalizer." (In his latest incarnation, venerable Eric was a crazy actor, scarred by fire while free-basing cocaine, and . . . well, you get the picture.)

In fact, some story lines are just too good to die. Take *Romeo and Juliet*, for instance. Penned by you-know-who in the Elizabethan era, it returned to sweep the Oscars back in 1961, as *West Side Story*. Twenty-six years later, it was back again with yet another ethnic twist, as *China Girl*. And while we're being honest, I must publicly acknowledge my own obligation to the Bard. In 1981, the editors of Carousel Books approached me with a problem: One of their authors had defaulted on a multiple-book contract, and they needed two Westerns in a hurry. In two weeks, to be precise. The titles were already carved in stone, but no one in the office had a clue about the plots, and so I borrowed Romeo and Juliet to write that sagebrush classic, *The Range War Nobody Won*. (What?! You missed it? Oh well, you're forgiven . . . *this* time.)

Like horror, Westerns, and the rest of genre fiction, action/adventure novels also fall back frequently on common, tested themes. If you've done any reading in the action genre — and you *should* have — you will recognize the old, time-honored themes on sight. You'll also recognize the difference between a common theme revived and plagiaristic hack-work ripping off the latest action movie or bestseller.

As a theme in literature, revenge has been around forever. *Moby Dick* is a revenge yarn, and despite the fact that college courses have been built around the "hidden symbolism" of the story, I suspect that Herman Melville — and his readers, too — were more contemporarily concerned with the adventure aspects of the tale, its pacing, and the monster waiting to make hash of Captain Ahab at the end. When Pendleton sat down to write *The Executioner*, he found a different twist for the revenge theme, and he thus made genre history. A host of copycats include some jewels, like *Rolling Thunder* and *The Shrewsdale Exit*, in the general glut of vigilante look-alikes.

The tale of Cain and Abel, pitting relatives or one-time friends against each other, is another proven theme, complete with undertones of vengeance and betrayal. Civil War fiction overflows with sundered families, divided loyalties, but fresh angles are still discovered occasionally, as in *The Killer Elite* and *Extreme Prejudice*.

Chase stories are a staple of the action genre, both in print and on the silver screen. Whole TV series, from "The Fugitive" to "Werewolf," have been based around the theme of hot pursuit, and director Walter Hill has made a career out of elegantly choreographed chase movies: *The Warriors*, *Southern Comfort*, *48 Hrs.*, *Streets of Fire*. Novels like my own *Paradine's Gauntlet* and *Run to Ground* (Gold Eagle, 1983 and 1987) continue the tradition, and it shows no sign of burning out as a potential source of story lines.

Closely allied to the chase theme is the quest for missing loved ones, usually abducted and in peril. Single titles like *The Children's Game*, *Night of the Juggler*, and *Stolen Flower* explore the boundaries of this theme, but it is also used, without spectacular success, in some protracted

27

series. *The Survivalist*, the *Night Hunter*, and the *M.I.A. Hunter* series all revolve around recovery of missing relatives or friends, and each inevitably stumbles on the fact that endless searching wears out both the hunter and the readers who attempt to follow in his footsteps.

Barring inspiration and a wholly new idea for this or that exciting tale, the would-be author's task is to identify the common themes that he or she can work with most effectively. Beyond that point, if you are worth your salt, imagination makes the story personally and uniquely yours. Before you're ready to approach that hurdle, though, there's still more homework to be done. You've got to read, read, read.

Learning from the Competition

I automatically assume that would-be writers come prepared and widely read within their chosen genre, having sampled both the classics and assorted stinkers in an effort to identify contemporary market trends, absorb the common elements of style, and profit from mistakes of their competitors by learning which snafus they should avoid. It's not enough to be a rabid fan, however. Reading *outside* the genre is equally vital for authors who wish to broaden their interests and perspective, sample common themes and their handling by other wordsmiths, or pick up pointers on plotting, characterization, and style.

Every avid reader has a list of favorite authors, and I'm not about to enter a debate on the relative merits of Harold Robbins versus James Michener or V. C. Andrews. I *will* recommend the following sixteen authors, for reasons specified below. If you have sampled and digested work from each of them, you're on the road to building an appreciation (and an understanding) of modern popular fiction. (Incidentally, my choices have been listed alphabetically, without regard to merit, so no ruffled feathers, please.)

Clive Barker is the new kid on the block in horror, working out of England through short stories—collected in his six-volume *Books of Blood* series—and novels like *The Damnation Game*. Barker's frank approach to sex and violence in his chosen genre may be hard for squeamish readers to accept, but if you're *that* soft, maybe you should give some second thoughts to picking out another genre . . . like romance, for instance. Any way you slice him, Barker is relentlessly original, with stories like "Son of Celluloid" and "Skins of the Fathers" breaking new ground in his field.

28

Robert Daley is a contemporary master of the police procedural, drawing upon personal experience with the N.Y.P.D. to produce compelling portraits of big-city cops, their families, friends, and adversaries. His best work to date is found in *Year of the Dragon*, but you shouldn't overlook such entries as *Hands of a Stranger*, either. While you're at it, keep an eye on Daley's characters, their development, and his insider's view of the New York Police Department, warts and all.

The late Ian Fleming came close to scooping Don Pendleton as the father of modern action/adventure, but his continental style and British point of view prevented him from kicking off a revolution in the States. If you're familiar with Fleming's James Bond only from the movies, and then primarily from Roger Moore's portrayal of the role, you owe it to yourself to read the original novels. It's amazing how well *Diamonds Are Forever*, *Moonraker*, and the rest of Fleming's stories stand up on their own, without the sci-fi trappings that directors ladle on to satisfy a jaded audience.

Ken Follett is a modern master of historical adventure, blending fact with fiction in such works as *The Key to Rebecca* and *The Eye of the Needle*. He's no slouch at nonfiction, either, but his forte clearly lies in action yarns, exotic settings . . . and, perhaps, nostalgia for the "good old days" of World War II.

Nobody—I repeat, nobody—weaves a plot like Frederick Forsyth. Each and every one of several dozen loose ends comes together for a rousing climax in his work, and Forsyth's novels stand as the epitome of "mainstream" action writing. From his debut, with *Day of the Jackal*, through blockbusters like *The Odessa File*, *The Dogs of War*, *The Fourth Protocol*, and *The Devil's Alternative*, Forsyth has been keeping readers on the edge of their seats and giving them double their money's worth in action, suspense, and intrigue.

Ex-journalist Thomas Harris broke on the literary scene with his novel *Black Sunday*, depicting a Palestinian terrorist attack on the Super Bowl, and followed up with the definitive portrait of a psychopathic serial killer in *Red Dragon*. His characters are finely drawn, his action scenes well-crafted, and my only strong criticism of Harris is that he does not publish more frequently.

Jack Higgins is a contemporary master of mainstream adventure, frequently weaving Irish rebels and their politics into bestsellers like *Confessional* and *A Prayer for the Dying*. He has also been successful at adapting real-life historical incidents as the basis for adventure stories—*Night of the Fox* and *The Eagle Has Landed* serve as two cases in point. Higgins's style is rather simplistic in comparison to that of Forsyth or Harris, but who ever said adventure writing had to be convoluted? Beginners could do worse than studying this writer's clear, straightforward prose.

Unless you've spent the past few years in a cave, I will assume you've heard of Stephen King. Pigeonholed by fans and critics as a "horror writer," King transcends the supernatural genre in short stories like "The Woman in the Room," novellas like *The Body* (filmed as *Stand By Me*), and full-length novels such as *Road Work*, *Rage*, or *Misery*. King spends considerable time on the creation of his homey characters, and he employs a master's touch in making stories come alive through the insertion of familiar, brand-name objects. Imitators have gone overboard, their novels reading more like long commercials for assorted household items, but when King portrays a character sipping Buckhorn beer and ogling the old Orange Crush thermometer, his readers *see* the poor, dumb schmuck; they *hear* that monster creeping up behind him, ravenous, insatiable.

Dean Koontz, like King, has been unfairly labeled as a "horror writer," with the implication that he can (or should) do nothing else. An "overnight success" in fiction who has worked for twenty years to make his name a household word, Koontz is best known for novels such as *Whispers*, *Phantoms*, and *Strangers*. Along the way, he has produced more than forty other books, including science fiction, poetry, and nonfiction. Would-be genre writers can learn much from Koontz in terms of plotting, building characters, and charting action scenes.

Speaking of labels, you probably knew Louis L'Amour as a prolific "Western writer." Well, guess again. Aside from riding with the Sacketts to determine how the West was won, L'Amour published several detective yarns and action-packed collections of stories set in World War II. Across the board, his trademark was definitive research, combining fact and fiction in a winning package. If L'Amour's top gun is carrying a Remington .44-40, you can bet the weapon will be described in loving—and factual—detail.

The tales of horror and suspense produced by Richard Laymon aren't for everyone, I grant you, but you'll never know for sure unless you give the guy a chance. A writer who delivers on the promise of a swift, hot read, Laymon's early work was trimmed of excess fat to the extent that certain elements of plot go unexplained, but minor deficits in logic are forgiven when the story packs a wallop. Laymon delivers a roundhouse punch in early novels like *The Cellar* and *The Woods Are Dark*, developing finesse in later volumes like *Tread Softly* and *Beware*. Explicit sex and violence keep the story rolling, and regardless of your ultimate assessment—love this writer's work or loathe it—you will find important pointers in the area of break-neck pacing and suspense.

I'm not a special fan of Robert Ludlum's work, but I include him here in deference to his impact on the espionage and suspense markets in modern fiction. Once you pare away the heavy prose and histrionics—"God damn this goddamned world!" etc., ad infinitum—you are treated to a view of complex plots, replete with violent action and intrigue. I would advise the cautious student to examine novels like *The Parsifal Mosaic* with an eye toward both the author's strengths and weaknesses, recalling that a reader lost around page 2 or 3 will not be with you for the brilliant climax you've prepared on page 300.

Martin Cruz Smith is another "overnight success" who made his bones with genre work, graduating to the best-seller lists with *Nightwing* and *Gorky Park*. The latter, just in case you missed it, is a fascinating inside view of Russia, offered through a Soviet policeman's eyes. It was a fresh idea when Smith conceived it, and the finished product stands as a reminder that occasionally authors should climb out on shaky limbs to chase their dreams.

Shane Stevens makes my list by virtue of a single novel, *By Reason of Insanity*. Intricate plotting and finely-drawn characters lift this story of a psycho-on-the-loose above its genre origins and make it a classic piece of modern suspense fiction. We know everything there is to know about his characters before the author wraps his story, and he *still* has the temerity to add a tight twist ending that will knock your socks off. Read this classic through for fun, and then go back to study its construction when the shock wears off.

No author in the modern period has had such striking influence on fantasy fiction as J. R. R. Tolkien. His alternate universe, devised in *The Hobbit* and carried on through *The Lord of the Rings* trilogy, is self-contained and consistent in every detail. Modern action writers generally will not be called upon to fabricate surrealistic landscapes or alien races, but it never hurts to watch a consummate word-magician at work. If you can give your "real-life" characters the spark and drive of Tolkien's orcs and hobbits, you will be a long stride down the road toward ultimate success.

Last but certainly not least in my compendium of favorite authors, Joseph Wambaugh does for L.A.'s finest what Robert Daley does for New York police . . . and Wambaugh does it even better. An experienced policeman at the time he wrote *The New Centurions*, Wambaugh brings an earthy flavor and an inside feel to his examinations of police in Southern California. I personally get more from his fiction than his forays into factual reporting, but throughout his work there is a feeling of involvement with policemen as they go about their daily work and watch The Job encroach upon their private lives. If nothing else, you should read Wambaugh for an honest look at how cops think and talk to one another, on and off the job.

By now, I hope you've gathered that there's more to genre writing—more to *any* writing—than just dreaming up a story and committing it to paper, willy-nilly. Skilled professionals make storytelling look so easy because (a) it comes as naturally to them as breathing, and (b) they've done their homework, paid their dues.

When you've done all *your* homework and decided on the basic sort of story you would like to tell, you're ready to proceed and take a shot at the construction of your novel. With a story line in mind, the plotting should be simple, right?

Well, not exactly. . . .

4. The Tangled Web

Assuming that you have a story line in mind, it's time to take that germ of an idea and build a working plot. I've got some good news and some bad news here.

The bad news first: For those of you who planned on breaking in with one or more short pieces, guess again. Before we take another step, you'll need to let your mind expand and think in terms of book-length stories. Yep, that's right—a *novel*.

As I mentioned back in Chapter 1, the classic marketplace for short adventure fiction, dubbed "the pulps," does not exist today. The macho magazines like *Stag* and *Men's Adventure*, popular throughout the fifties and the early sixties, are a fading memory. I miss them on occasion, but the fact is that they're dead and gone. Unless the art form makes a comeback—and there's been no indication of it in a quarter-century—adventure writers with a short attention span are out of luck.

I won't say it's *impossible* to place a short adventure piece, and if you find a ready market I'd appreciate a tip, but a review of current options offers little room for hope. Men's magazines like *Cavalier* and *Chic* may advertise for short "adventure" fiction, but they haven't come within a mile of hard-core genre stock since *Playboy* serialized Ian Fleming's last novels in the James Bond series twenty years ago. Horror and fantasy magazines likewise hold no promise, unless your fiction has a sci-fi twist like *Predator*—and that's been done, in case you haven't noticed. The handful of mystery magazines generally prefer more sedate fare, minimizing blood and gore in favor of cerebral exercises, and magazines like *Soldier of Fortune* concentrate on nonfiction reports. Comics publishers may be

33

your last, best hope, but most demand accompanying artwork with the stories they acquire.

Okay, you've heard the bad news.

The good news is: The thought of tackling a novel should not prove intimidating to a real professional. If you can plot a short piece, chances are that you can also plot a novel. The construction of a working plot is fairly simple and straightforward if you keep the basic, mandatory elements in mind.

Bare Essentials

For openers, your story—*any* story—must have *conflict*. If you have a story line in mind, you've got your basic conflict covered, going in—and if you don't, you've got no business trying to construct a plot in any case. Your conflict is the major problem facing your protagonist(s), which he (or she, or they) must solve before the story's end. Your hero may be trying to prevent a terrorist assassination, crack a drug ring, rescue hostages, or find the missing link—whatever. Conflict is a story's launching pad; without it, you have nothing.

If you haven't sorted out your basic conflict yet, go back to Chapter 3 and try again. Do not pass "Go." Do not collect your royalty checks.

From basic conflict, you evolve a string of *complications*, incidents and obstacles that will prevent a quick solution to the story's central problem. If your hero is confronted by a villain and he settles all their hassles with a single punch, you haven't got a story. At the very most, you're working on an anecdote, which may be great for filler in the *Reader's Digest*, but it won't a novel make.

Remember that a *short* adventure novel, based on current market standards, runs approximately 60,000 words in length. Most weigh in closer to 75,000 words at press time, and the more substantial entries start right around 100,000 words. Don't get me wrong: I'm not suggesting you begin with manuscripts of Ludlumesque proportions, and you shouldn't throw in pointless scenes of sex and violence for the sake of padding, either. (Editors *will* notice). Action writing should be lean and tight, but there is also such a thing as literary anorexia, and writers who consistently fall short of fleshing out their stories may expect to go unpublished while they learn their craft.

I have been privileged—if that's the word—to scrutinize a number of the action manuscripts that would-be authors send off to Gold Eagle's editors from time to time. We're talking *unsolicited* submissions here, the kind that feed the slush pile, and while some may have potential, most are best described as . . . odd. The worst I've seen, hand-written, took a single sheet of foolscap paper to describe protagonists and villains, set the stage for action, and conduct a ninja showdown, getting everyone off-stage before the author literally reached his bottom line. In case you're wondering, this "novel" didn't sell—and I suspect the writer wonders why.

The moral: If your story gets *too* lean, it disappears.

A story's payoff is delivered in the *climax* and/or *resolution*, when the hero has his showdown with the heavies and their conflict is resolved, for good or ill. (A happy ending isn't absolutely mandatory, but you should remember not to kill off your hero if you anticipate a sequel!) I should note that, while a story's climax and its resolution travel hand in hand, they are not necessarily synonymous. The *climax* is your story's turning point, the pinnacle of action, but it need not be the final scene, in which loose ends are neatly tied together.

Lowering the Boom

Various successful authors place climactic moments *near* the end—or even in the middle—of their novels, winding down to laid-back resolutions that may cover several pages, even several chapters, while the characters relax or lick their wounds, make love, and generally put their lives in order. In *Casino Royale*, James Bond's showdown with Le Chiffre is planted near the middle of a relatively slim adventure; afterward, Bond spends some time in the hospital, and then embarks on a vacation with his lady of the moment, luscious Vesper Lynd. A similar, though shorter, convalescent period is used to good effect by Thomas Harris in *Red Dragon*, following the second "death" of killer Francis Dolarhyde. And in the field of epic fantasy—*The Stand*, *Lord of the Rings*, *Swan Song*—hefty chunks of prose are frequently devoted to assuring readers that the heroes' lives are back on track.

Conversely, in a streamlined action novel, climax may collide and coincide with resolution to complete the story in a single stroke. A prime example may be found in the work of Mickey Spillane, where hard-boiled detective yarns typically end with the pull of the trigger, destroying the villain before nosy coppers and lawyers arrive on the scene. I sometimes use the technique myself, when a fast wrap appears to suit everyone's needs. In *Blood Dues* (Gold Eagle, 1984), for instance, the books close on Cuban agent Jorge Ybarra at an embassy party in Miami:

> *His eyes narrowed against the sudden glare, and he discerned something on his desk, a bulky object . . . not unlike a football. He took a closer step, frowning . . . and he recognized the head of Raoul Ornelas, wide eyes gaping at him sightlessly, the mouth twisted into one last grimace, hair matted down with blood.*
>
> *Ybarra felt the scream rising in his throat, but vomit choked it off. He was gagging, backing away from the desk on unsteady legs, when a subtle scraping sound behind him alerted him to danger.*
>
> *He spun around, mouth dropping open at the sight of a tall man, dressed in skintight black, emerging from behind the office door. The intruder's face was blackened with cosmetics, eyes as cold as death itself — and the automatic pistol in his rising fist was silencer-equipped.*
>
> *Jorge Ybarra never heard the shot that killed him.*

At the close of *The Fiery Cross* (Gold Eagle, 1988), Mack Bolan takes a Russian sleeper agent on a one-way ride:

> *Locking the front door behind him, he strode briskly down the walk, across his lawn, in the direction of the waiting limousine. A different driver held the door for Andrews, smiling deferentially, and he supposed that Thomas must have called in sick. No matter. Nothing could be less significant than the selection of a new chauffeur.*
>
> *He settled back into the leather-upholstered seat, contemplating the future with mounting enthusiasm. Somewhere tropical, perhaps — at least for openers. And later, Switzerland. Or Liechtenstein. Perhaps the Orient.*
>
> *He missed the usual landmarks, did not recognize the storefronts sliding past his tinted window. Leaning forward, he pressed the button on the intercom that linked him with the driver.*
>
> *"Why are we going this way? Thomas never comes this way."*
>
> *The driver's eyes were studying him, not without a trace of curiosity, in the rearview mirror.*
>
> *"Short cut," said the Executioner, before he put the pedal to the floor.*

From time to time, protagonists can even sit the final action out, off-stage. The conclusion of *The Trial* (Gold Eagle, 1986) focuses on the major heavy, rancher Ethan Peck, and his comeuppance in the fallout from an unsuccessful bid to frame the story's hero on a murder charge:

> *He felt the pistol's weight tugging at his belt, inviting him to try his hand. It would be suicidal, certainly. The scattergun was pointed at his chest, and he could never hope to beat the gunner's time. It was preposterous. Insane.*
>
> *And it was still the only game in town.*
>
> *He knew the Duke would try it in his place. The Duke would never have surrendered to some snot-nosed city boy, no matter if the snot-nose had a cannon leveled at his chest.*
>
> *"You ever go to movies, boy?"*
>
> *The snot-nose looked confused, but he was holding steady on the scattergun, his knuckle white with tension on the trigger. Counting down his life in microseconds now, the rancher knew precisely what he had to do.*
>
> *And he was grinning when he made his move.*

Whichever way you go — the guillotine approach or a more leisurely retreat — your resolution must provide the reader with at least a semblance of reality and logic. If you plan on letting Mother Nature take your heavies out with a convenient avalanche or tidal wave — or, as in *Balefire*, with a killer shark that turns up in an early chapter and again at the conclusion, with no visible connection between the two events — you might be wise to brace yourself for a rejection.

Outlines vs. Inspiration

Working authors universally approach their goal — a finished novel — via one of two established routes. A goodly number chart their stories with the help of outlines, while another faction trusts in what I like to call the "crisis method." Many writers — and some damned successful ones, at that — are loathe to plot their stories in advance, abhorring the "restrictions" of an outline or synopsis, falling back on mood and inspiration while the story "writes itself."

37

Don Pendleton, creator of *The Executioner*, occasionally wrote his hero into corners, literally trusting dreams to furnish the solutions. In *Panic in Philly* (Pinnacle, 1973), Mack Bolan is up a phone pole, tapping Mafia lines, when police materialize below. He's cornered, sworn to never shoot a cop, and Pendleton admittedly had no ideas for his escape until, he says, the black-clad warrior turned up in a dream. No words were spoken; Bolan merely sat and stared, but Pendleton awoke with an abiding urge to hit the keyboard of his IBM. The answer? Bolan detonates explosives in his van, parked up the street, by means of a remote control switch on his belt, then leaps to safety in a nearby tree while everyone is scattering for cover.

Four years later, in the midst of *Savage Fire* (Pinnacle, 1977), Don walked his hero — posing as a mobster — into the heart of an enemy stronghold. No one on earth can see through his disguise, except perhaps for Augie Marinello, a *capo mafioso* blasted and presumed dead in an earlier episode. As Don explained to me, "I had no idea who would be in that room when Bolan walked in, but it turned out to be Augie." This time, a swan dive through the nearest window saves the day, but only after Bolan triggers rockets, launched via remote control from his nearby "warwagon," to intercept the gunners on his tail.

Don Pendleton is not alone in hewing to the "crisis method" in his work. Prolific horror writer Ramsey Campbell gets by with a brief synopsis, which he uses merely as a "safety net," preferring "to let the novel develop itself as it takes on more life." No less a paragon than Stephen King has branded outlines as "the refuge of bad fiction writers," but he didn't hesitate to use one for his preparation of *The Talisman*, with Peter Straub, in 1981.

Most pros would no more think of sitting down to write without *some* kind of outline than they would consider driving coast-to-coast without a map, or going naked to the local supermarket. J. N. Williamson, who has completed thirty-seven books in a decade, states (in *How to Write Tales of Horror, Fantasy & Science Fiction*) that, "Good plots . . . happen, more often than not, because of well-planned outlines." John Gardner does not sneer at inspiration, but he still contends (in *On Becoming a Novelist*) that, "Sooner or later the writer has no choice but to figure out what he's doing." Veteran mystery editor Barbara Norville regards a detailed outline, prepared in three or four stages, as "the backbone of the book" (*Writing the Modern Mystery*). Ken Follett has revealed, in published interviews, that he outlines each book repeatedly, inserting greater detail as he goes, incorporating character descriptions, bits of dialogue, whole action scenes, until the final product reaches 30,000 words or more! With outline in hand, he begins to write, and finds it necessary to revise his manuscript only once—compared to an average two or three drafts claimed by Stephen King.

I personally would not care to start on any book without a clear idea of where the plot and characters are going. I may not adhere religiously to the initial outline—massive chunks may be revised or cast aside before I'm finished—but *at least it's there*. So far—knock wood—I haven't found myself out thrashing in the darkness, flirting with disaster (not to mention writer's block) while waiting for a dream to solve the riddle of a crucial character's survival.

There are several clear advantages to working from an outline. First, it helps you keep your characters and story line on track, reducing opportunities for meaningless digression. Action stories *move*, and while an editor won't fault you for developing your characters, providing background and the like, you can't afford too many of the famous Ian Fleming thirty-five-page gourmet meals or golf games, either. It is also possible to lose a character, from time to time, in the excitement of the chase. (I've done it once or twice, but I console myself with memories of Dirty Harry Callahan, who can't remember if he's fired six shots . . . or only five.) These kinds of technical snafus are easily avoided if you keep a weather eye on your synopsis as you work.

Another benefit of using outlines is elimination of the "do or die" mentality that hovers over writers working by the crisis method. If you've sketched your hero's movements in advance, you won't be forced to hurl him out of seventh-story windows, praying that a too-convenient awning will be waiting for him down below. It usually shows when writers let their stories take them by surprise, and the "solutions" they contrive to unexpected hazards often come out sounding corny and contrived, if not downright cartoonish. It may not hurt your hero's reputation to rely on Fate for his salvation once or twice—I'm talking once or twice within a *series*, not a single story—but if he or she habitually blunders into peril unprepared, you're dealing with a clumsy idiot.

Aside from helping out with characters and sticky situations, outlines let a writer pace a story properly, and they can also help with *sales*. Most editors (and many agents) don't have time to wade through stacks of unsolicited manuscripts, but they often insist upon a finished outline or synopsis, which includes the ending of your story. Unless you're Norman Mailer, pulling down $4 million for the mere announcement that you have a book in mind, don't plan on selling anyone a pig in a poke. Editors will want to *see* your story, verify the logic of its resolution, and be certain that it hasn't been done countless times before by other writers.

Working Outlines

The synopsis you submit to editor or agent may take several forms, and we'll discuss particulars of the submission at a later point. For now, I've reproduced below an outline for an episode of the *Executioner* series, which was purchased by Gold Eagle Books in 1988, as *Night Kill*.

We open with a human sacrifice in progress, the intended victim drugged in preparation for the deed. In spite of her sedation, she is vaguely conscious of the hooded figures circling a makeshift altar where she lies spread-eagle, as an offering to Satan. Although terrified, she is unable to resist, and consciousness deserts her as the high priest draws his knife, the blade descending. . . .

Join Mack Bolan as he keeps a date arranged by Hal Brognola. Mack is meeting Amos Carr, an ex-policeman presently employed as a consultant in the field of cult-related crime. A self-taught expert, drawn to study Satanists and other fringe religions by his own experience with groups which prey upon impressionable youngsters, Carr is tracking what he thinks may be a nationwide Satanic network, linked to human sacrifices in a dozen cities, trafficking in drugs and child pornography while wooing countless teenagers through messages included in the lyrics of Satanic "heavy metal" tunes. The Executioner is skeptical at first, but Carr has slides, police reports, the affidavits of defectors and survivors, all apparently connecting "random" murders with the travels of a leading heavy metal band, "Apocalypse."

By no coincidence, the band is playing that same evening, in the town Carr has selected for his meet with Bolan. They check out the action, Bolan alternately fascinated and repulsed by what he hears and sees. The audience is whipped into a frenzy by their heroes on the stage, and Carr fills Bolan in on the connection of the singers to a noted author (and Satanic "priest") named Lucian Slate, who travels with them on retainer as their counselor and "spiritual guide."

Meanwhile, on the other side of town, a rather different sort of gathering is underway. Televangelist Jordan Braithwaite has brought his salvation road show to the city, hot on the heels of Apocalypse and their message of darkness. As we meet Braithwaite, he is preaching hellfire and communing with the Holy Ghost on wavelengths only he can tap, producing wild reactions from his audience and "healing" carefully-selected shills to keep the money flowing as collection plates are passed.

Before the night is over, there will be another sacrificial murder of a teenaged girl — a member of the heavy metal audience which heard Apocalypse perform short hours earlier. Next morning, Carr and Bolan view the crime scene, rubbing shoulders with police, who are predominantly hostile to the notion of Satanic cultists in their midst. They would prefer to blame a "normal maniac," but one or two have heard Carr's message in the past, and they are starting to believe.

Carr introduces Bolan to an ally, Cassandra Poole, a "white" witch who takes her religion seriously and despises practitioners of the black arts. She has worked with Carr before, and agrees to brief Bolan on the local occult scene, giving him pointers on which groups to watch for and which it is safe to ignore. Her briefing extends into a tour of local occult bookshops and supply stores, with introductions to a few practitioners, while Carr strikes off on business of his own. When they regroup, Carr mentions the "coincidence" of Jordan Braithwaite's appearance in cities where Apocalypse has played and victims have been slain. It may be nothing more than shrewd publicity, but Bolan is no great believer in coincidence.

While Bolan trails Cassandra to a meeting of her coven, delving

41

deeper into the occultic scene, we meet Satanic hit man Owen York, a veteran of the Manson days and unidentified participant in New York's "Son of Sam" assassinations, lately on the payroll of an underground "black" network spanning the United States. A zealous worshipper, York is a pragmatist, as well. His roving team of killers love their work, but they are also in it for the money they are paid by Lucian Slate and his clandestine backers.

As Bolan, Carr, and beautiful Cassandra work the underground in search of suspects, they are also setting off alarms, alerting York and Slate to danger in the wind. Apocalypse has one more gig to play before they hit the road, and Slate decrees that any snoopers who cannot be frightened off must die, before they ruin everything. A phony lead lures Amos Carr into an ambush, but he battles clear and races off to warn the others of impending danger. He comes too late for Cass, arriving as York's cronies carry her away, and Carr is wounded when he tries to intervene. He will survive, and Bolan's hasty meeting with the injured man is all he needs to make him join the band, backstage.

A Bolan heart-to-heart with the Apocalypse musicians leads him to the site where Cass is scheduled to be sacrificed. The Executioner's arrival foils York's plan, resulting in the deaths of Slate and his accomplices. Before he dies, however, Slate will name his secret financier and boss as "Reverend" Braithwaite. An unprincipled manipulator, con man, and prospective politician on a "Christian" platform, Braithwaite has employed the Satanists much as he uses phony cripples in his own revivals—to create a mood, provoke desired responses from his audience, and bring the masses "back to God" . . . or, in this case, to Jason Braithwaite.

In the final chapter, Bolan pays a visit to the reverend, sending Braithwaite on to meet his maker—whom, we may suspect, is not amused. An epilogue finds Amos mending nicely, and perhaps the Executioner can spare some time for Cass, to search for magic of a different kind.

Within the space of roughly three typed pages, double-spaced, I've set the story rolling with an action scene, delineated major characters, and laid out every major action scene from the appearance of our hero through the climax and a quasi-happy ending. (Inspiration for the story, incidentally, was drawn from recent media reports on Satanism and the feet of clay displayed by leading televangelists.) That general framework gave me ample room to throw my characters some gruesome curves and keep the readers guessing—just so long as *I* was never in the dark.

Okay, this isn't English 101; you're not required to use an outline, and assuming that you do, there are no hard, fast rules about the form you should employ. I do not recommend the rigid outlines taught in school, with Roman numerals and whatnot, as the basis for a novel, though they come in handy on occasion for nonfiction work. The plain fact is that if you're wise and talented enough to be a writer in the first place, you can choose the kind of outline or synopsis that works best for you.

In length and structure, working outlines range from Follett's 30,000-word novellas to the simpler, much shorter version shown above. J. N. Williamson suggests a breakdown of the outline into chapters, while Ray Obstfeld—author of *The Warlord* series and assorted other novels—advocates the "slap-dash" outline, breaking up a story into scenes, with brief descriptions of the action found in each. Once I've progressed beyond a sales pitch to the actual production of a finished manuscript, I use a hybrid of the latter methods, laying out my story in sequential chapters, plotting sketchy scenes within each segment, finally putting meat and sinew on the bones when I sit down to write.

Production of a useful working outline should not be a problem if you follow certain basic steps. First off, you'll need to brainstorm, starting with a general story line in mind and letting your imagination run until it's tired, creating characters and coughing up scenarios that meet your needs. At this point, you're collecting anything and everything; there's time enough to cut the dead wood later, when your plot has taken shape.

Sketch profiles of your major characters as they appear, and write them down. The names aren't crucial yet; a simple "A" or "B" will do, as long as you can start to picture them and get a feel for who they are, their personalities, perversions, quirks, and foibles. Scribble down the physical descriptions if you're moved to do so—anything from height and hair and eyes, to scars, tattoos, peculiar accents. If you're dealing with a pyromaniac who shaves his head and loves vanilla ice cream, you should know it going in.

Jot down your various scenarios on index cards, including any details you can think of. "A shoots B" may say it all for now, or you may have a special gun in mind, a certain setting that will make or break the scene. If bits of dialogue present themselves, go on and write them down; six months from now, that snappy phrase may not be rattling around inside your head precisely when you need it. Don't concern yourself with linking scenes together or compiling them in order at this point; we're free-associating here, and if you try to run straight through the story start-to-finish on your first time out, I'm betting that you'll choke. (*I* do, invariably.) In the end, some scenes will work while others fail; a few will be discarded altogether, fresh ones added in their place, but none of this should faze you while you're still in brainstorm mode.

When your creative process finally stalls, it's time to sort the index cards and put your various scenarios in some apparent order. Certain bits may naturally place themselves — a perfect prologue, or the major heavy's death scene, for example — but you'll find that many more are flexible. Each separate card need not a chapter make; a handful may be merged, or one may be expanded into several chapters. You're the boss.

You may have dreamed up subplots that no longer function logically within the living story, and if so, you must be ruthless, amputating those that don't belong. Conversely, gaps will almost certainly appear at points within the outline, begging to be filled with characters and action. Two scenarios that didn't fit together previously may work out, provided that you find a proper bridge. Ideally, filler for the gaps should make some contribution to the gathering momentum of the story. Simple padding — sex and violence thrown in randomly to make a word-count — is among the quickest ways to see your book go up in flames. (Remember all the times you've felt ripped off by cheapo exploitation films, with pointless shower scenes included merely to display some skin? Same principle, except that here, your editor may holler "Cut!" before the readers have a chance to feel ripped off.)

Delineating Chapters

When it came time for me to write *Night Kill*, I broke my short synopsis down as follows, making it a useful working outline.

44

NIGHT KILL

Cast: Mack Bolan
      Amos Carr—ex-cop, consultant on Satanic cults
      Cassandra Poole—a "white" witch, friend of Carr's
      Lucian Slate—occult celebrity, advisor to "Apocalypse"
      Owen York—ex-Mansonite, Satanic killer, works for
            Slate
      Jordan Braithwaite—televangelist in league with
            Satanists
      "Apocalypse" band members—
       1. Clay Deatheridge, aka "Death": lead singer
       2. Mike O'Neal, aka "Skull": lead guitar
       3. Freddy Sykes, aka "Ripper": bass guitar
       4. Tommy Piersall, aka "Ax": keyboards
       5. John Beamish, aka "Mephisto": drums

Outline:
    Prologue—Open w/ sacrificial murder of young groupie
    Ch. 1—Bolan meets Amos, gets briefing; they go to concert
    Ch. 2—Split POVs w/ "Apocalypse" in concert
    Ch. 3—Split POVs, across town, at Braithwaite's revival
    Ch. 4—Sacrifice of groupie from the new concert audience
    Ch. 5—Bolan/Amos at murder scene; interact w/ cops
    Ch. 6—Amos takes Bolan to meet Cass, discuss local cults
    Ch. 7—Intro. Slate, holding ritual for band members
    Ch. 8—Split POVs: Amos solo; Bolan/Cass tour under-
           ground
    Ch. 9—Regroup w/ Amos; hear Braithwaite on radio
    Ch. 10—Intro. York + team at 2nd concert, picking victims
    Ch. 11—Split POVs: Bolan attends "white" coven w/ Cass
    Ch. 12—Braithwaite meets Slate; payoff + strategy session
    Ch. 13—W/York in graveyard ritual; b.g. + interiors
    Ch. 14—Split POVs: Cass solo, accidentally alerting York
    Ch. 15—Split POVs: Slate + York move against "snoopers"
    Ch. 16—Amos lured into ambush; escapes + goes to Cass
    Ch. 17—Cass snatched by York; Amos wounded, warns
           Bolan
    Ch. 18—Bolan grills members of "Apocalypse" for info.

Ch. 19/20—Showdown w/ cultists; York rats on Braithwaite
Ch. 21—Bolan settles accounts w/ Braithwaite
Epilogue—Visit Amos in hospital; split w/ Cass for "R&R"

This simple, one-page outline was the backbone for a novel exceeding 75,000 words in length. The notations "b.g." and "interiors" in Chapter 13 refer to insertion of background and interior viewpoints for a specific character, of which more, later. Various notations of "Split POVs" refer to chapters I planned to subdivide, approaching crucial scenes from several different points of view.

As I approach each chapter in its turn, I normally prepare a much-abbreviated "slap-dash" outline of the major action. Thus, for Chapter 8, I might prepare a sketch as follows:

Ch. 8—Split POVs:
  A) Amos interviews his contacts in the underground
  B) Cass leads Bolan on a tour of occult shops + hangouts
  C) Magic shop proprietor phones contacts to report that "someone" is investigating "black" practitioners

---

Each scene will be approached from a distinct and separate point of view, resulting in a chapter that should tip the scales around four thousand words. There is no mandatory word-count for a given scene, of course, but publishers will generally specify that finished manuscripts must reach a certain minimum in words (or pages) to fulfill your contract. Falling short by several thousand words—or several dozen pages—will result in calls for rewrites and additions, which may prove extremely awkward once you've put a tale to bed. It's easier, and more professional, to pace yourself on works in progress, feeding in material that meets the story's needs.

(This *doesn't* mean that you should pad your script outrageously by throwing in the kitchen sink on every scene. If you are working on a contract that demands a manuscript of 60,000 words, don't send the editor a thousand pages of material. He won't appreciate the "bonus," doesn't need the eye strain, and his budget probably will not accommodate a book that makes the Bible look like D.C. Comics.)

Coherence, or the Problem of the Disappearing Heavy

Perhaps the most important single element of plotting is *coherence*. Mysteries are fine, and complicated subplots sometimes help a book if you can pull them off, but every action in your story must eventually make sense. It's fine to keep the motives of your characters a secret *for a while*, but if the curtain never rises on a logical solution, editors will probably suggest you spend a few more hours at the drawing board. Loose ends and unresolved conundrums don't make happy readers, and unhappy readers may be prone to spend their time (and money) with another author next time out.

Confession time. I once forgot to kill a major villain at the climax of a novel. Like the bullet-count in Dirty Harry's .44, he slipped my mind and got away in the confusion of the final showdown. I did not intend for him to get away, you understand; I simply lost him. No one noticed in the editorial department, and I didn't see the glitch myself, until the book was published. Everything worked out — I brought the hairball back and killed him in a sequel — but it left me with a feeling that I'd fumbled on the two-yard line and nearly blown the game.

"The Formula"

Whenever genre plotting is discussed, someone inevitably raises specters of "The Formula." Come on, you know the rap, where adding "X" and "Y" inevitably gives you "Z". Depending on your point of view, The Formula may be an easy ticket to the big-time, or an evil monster that prevents most genre writing from attaining elevation to the ranks of "literature."

We may as well face facts: The Formula exists. In every genre — be it action, Western, horror, mystery, romance — there are established plot conventions that your readers (and your critics) automatically expect to find in each and every tale. To some extent, the elements of formulaic writing may be unavoidable in genre fiction, but aspiring authors should not be intimidated — or enslaved — by the requirements of The Formula.

In basic terms, the formula for modern action/adventure includes (1) a strong protagonist, confronted by (2) some mortal threat from (3) selected heavies, leading to (4) a gruelling pursuit, resolved through (5) a violent confrontation or series of same. The pursuit can go either way, with your hero playing fox or hound as you prefer, but you must always finish strong.

(A former editor of my acquaintance once tried publishing a totally *nonviolent* action novel. Anybody care to guess why he's no longer in the business?)

If you think about it, you will see there's ample room for individuality within the basic recipe, but caution is required. If you desert the formula completely, readers may not recognize your work. Conversely, if you cling too slavishly to formula, you may discover that your stories all begin to sound alike.

Throughout his early years with Pinnacle, Don Pendleton was faced with editorial demands that he adhere to formula in the production of adventure novels. Heated calls demanding higher body-counts, more deaths per page, were not unusual, but for the most part Don stuck by his guns and wrote the stories *his* way, with a keen eye on ingredients that made *The Executioner* a hit in the beginning.

On the flip side, Ian Fleming was reduced to something like self-parody by his adherence to The Formula in writing James Bond stories. In his final full-length novel, *The Man with the Golden Gun*, Fleming fell back on the Caribbean setting familiar from two previous books—*Live and Let Die* and *Doctor No*—while incorporating the "hood's congress" from *Goldfinger* and the miniature train from *Diamonds Are Forever*. More derivative than inspirational, the tale is generally considered Fleming's least successful work.

Occasionally, you may find yourself confronted with an editor who worships at the feet of formula, demanding that your work adhere to certain rigid guidelines. Such conditions normally arise in work-for-hire agreements, dealing with production of a "house name" series such as *Longarm* or *Nick Carter*, where a team of writers grind out novels on a predetermined schedule, losing their identities in favor of a macho-sounding, nonexistent "author." The producers of one adult Western series are known for their insistence that writers include at least three sex scenes per manuscript (coupling the hero with a different woman for each encounter), and similar guidelines are often applied to action scenes. When I ghosted the first two novels in the *M.I.A. Hunter* series for Berkley-Jove in 1985, I had instructions to incorporate two martial arts encounters in each story. It was not a problem, and I did not feel creatively confined, but I present it here as an example of The Formula in action.

In all fairness, I should say that slavish adoration of The Formula is not a kiss of death, per se. John Saul has been producing carbon-copy novels in the horror market for a long, long time, and doing very well besides. You know the story: Once upon a time, a hundred years ago, something terrible happened in Anytown, U.S.A., and now it's happening *again*! There's a moral in here, somewhere, but I'm damned if I know what it is. Personally, if I knew my career was restricted to a single story, I'd shoot for *Gone with the Wind*, rather than a dozen cookie-cutter look-alikes of *Pee Wee's Big Adventure*.

The bottom line is this, my friends: A conscientious pro respects his readers *and* himself. He works within the strictures of his chosen genre, but he gives his talent and imagination room to ramble. *Quality* is still the standard authors must be judged by, in the end. A lazy writer may get by on flashy cover art until his readers find him out, but they *will* find him out. And all the Day-Glo paint there ever was won't help a rotten novel stand the acid test of audience approval.

5. The Hook

Every hero's quest commences with a single step, and so must every story have a starting point. If you get careless and misplace your readers on the first page of your novel, you can bet they won't be with you for the rousing climax.

Simply stated, then, you need a "hook" to catch and hold your audience, so you can reel them in. The hook has two important functions, one artistic and the other purely mercenary. Since we're talking business here, let's deal with money first.

Before you publish anything, you must impress an editor with your material, your style, your *talent*. This is where the bucks stop, literally. If prospective editors discover they can use your manuscript as an alternative to Sominex, you may as well forget about those paydays. No one — I mean *no one* — consciously sets out to foist a boring novel on the public. Editors will judge your work beginning with the first line that they read — in many cases, on the basis of your cover letters — and a conscientious pro makes every effort to secure a sale by leading with the good stuff.

Once you've got that contract in the bag, it's time to satisfy a broader audience. Remember that you have an active share in the promotion of your novel. Cover art and advertising copy may be all it takes for some, but I've been known to read the first page of a story standing in the supermarket, and I'll wager many others do the same. If that first paragraph is awkward, if it doesn't *grab* me, chances are I'll pass the author by and keep on looking.

Sharpening the Hook

Having said that much, what constitutes a "good" beginning? Obviously, that's subjective. One man's hook may be another's sleeper, but I think

51

we can arrive at some conclusions by comparing two examples.

In *The Slaughter Run* (Zebra, 1980), Axel Kilgore introduces both his story and his hero thus:

> *The wind was starting to blow up hard as Hank Frost stood on the brow of the isolated slope, watching the reddish orange orb of sun start to sink low toward the tree line, the pines offering what modest protection there was from the ice spicules pounding like tiny needles against the exposed skin of his cheeks and forehead. "At least my eyepatch will keep me warm," he said, but to no one in particular. Frost was alone — very alone — he thought, snapping away the butt of the burnt-to-the-fingertips Camel he'd been smoking while thinking about Bess. A plane was flying overhead, a commercial jet, but it was only in books and movies, he reflected, that as the hero stood on the icy mountaintop the heroine would be sitting wistfully aboard the aircraft flying overhead — lovers, star-crossed and so close but yet so far! He closed his thoughts by verbalizing the word, "Bullshit" and pulled his ski mask from the pocket of his jacket. Bess, he thought, though he loved her dearly, wasn't exactly the "wistful" type.*

This passage, plainly speaking, is a clunker, badly overweight with surplus adjectives and phrases shoe-horned in "for drama's sake." Compare it to the opening of *Gorky Park*, penned by Martin Cruz Smith:

> *All nights should be so dark, all winters so warm, all headlights so dazzling.*
>
> *The van jacked, stalled and quit on a drift, and the homicide team got out, militia officers cut from a pattern of short arms and low brows, wrapped in sheepskin greatcoats. The one not in uniform was a lean, pale man, the chief investigator. He listened sympathetically to the tale of the officer who had found the bodies in the snow: the man had only strayed so far from the park footpath in the middle of the night to relieve himself, then he saw them, himself half undone, as it were, and just about froze, too. The team followed the beam of the van's spotlight.*
>
> *The investigator suspected the poor dead bastards were just a vodka troika that had cheerily frozen to death. Vodka was liquid taxation, and the price was always rising. It was accepted that three was the lucky number on a bottle in terms of economic prudence and de-*

sired effect. It was a perfect example of primitive communism.

The prose employed by Smith is economical, dynamic, with an imagery as clear as crystal. By the time I finished reading that, I knew I'd buy his *next* book when it hit the stands. (I did, and it was great.)

Say What You Mean . . . Then Shut Up

Before you start to craft your perfect hook, you should decide precisely what you hope to do with the beginning of your story. Basically, you have three options: you can sketch a setting for your readers; you can introduce a character; or you can pick the story up in progress, with an action scene.

Whichever way you go, be sure to keep in mind two fundamental tenets. *Economy of language* is the first; Big Brother wasn't kidding when he told his followers that "less is more." If you can make your point with five words, why use thirty-five? I dare say Kilgore's flabby paragraph, examined earlier, could probably have been reduced to three or four short sentences with nothing lost—and reader interest salvaged. *Clarity* should be a central focus of your thoughts while writing. Picture every scene before you try describing it. If your descriptions come off sounding vague to *you*, how can a hapless stranger ever hope to muddle through? Precision and economy of language travel hand-in-hand.

Stage Settings

There are as many ways of setting up a scene as there are working writers in the business, but no matter how they do it, all the best pros manage to establish *moods* for every setting they describe. This goal can be achieved in many ways, with broad allowances for style. Let's take a look at some examples.

In *The Haunting of Hill House*, author Shirley Jackson opens her tale as follows:

> *No live organism can continue for long to exist sanely under con-*
> *ditions of absolute reality; even larks and katydids are supposed, by*
> *some, to dream. Hill House, not sane, stood by itself against its hills,*
> *holding darkness within; it had stood so for eighty years and might*

stand for eighty more. Within, walls continued upright, bricks met neatly, floors were firm, and doors were sensibly shut; silence lay steadily against the wood and stone of Hill House, and whatever walked there, walked alone.

This passage is a classic of economy and grace. Within three sentences, we find a brief description and a capsule history of Hill House, coupled with the chilling information that it is alive, insane, and probably inhabited by something we should leave alone. The author has immediately captured our attention and set the mood for nastiness to come, while dishing out one of the finest short descriptive passages in modern literature.

In "Red Wind," Raymond Chandler uses a stylish weather report to set the stage for future action with detective Philip Marlowe:

> *There was a desert wind blowing that night. It was one of those hot dry Santa Anas that come down through the mountain passes and curl your hair and make your nerves jump and your skin itch. On nights like that every booze party ends in a fight. Meek little wives feel the edge of the carving knife and study their husbands' necks. Anything can happen. You can even get a full glass of beer at a cocktail lounge.*

In "The Lake of the Left-Handed Moon," author Robert Leslie Bellem puts his hero on wheels for a memorable passage ripe with foreboding:

> *My tires sang a tune on the dark curves and the tune was a prelude to murder. I didn't know this at the time, of course. I knew only that the road climbed and twisted, with the mountains squeezing in on me as I tooled my jalopy up the inclined serpentine turns. Barring the merged cones of brilliance my headlamps made, I was surrounded by a blackness you could slice with a razor and get whittlings of coal.*

In *Houston Attack* (Dell, 1985), a title from the *Hawker* series, author Carl Ramm stages his opening south of the border:

> *The bar was on the Mexican side of the Rio Grande. It was built of concrete block on a concrete slab in a border town where the desert*

pressed hard against the slum housing and tequila joints.

The bar had once been painted a fluorescent green. But the Mexican sun had leached the color from it, and now, beneath its red neon sign, the building looked gray in the summer darkness.

Las Almas Desconocidas.

A fitting name for such a bar, thought James Hawker.

The Bar of the Unknown Souls.

In the sixty-seventh episode of their *Destroyer* series, *Look Into My Eyes* (Signet, 1986), Warren Murphy and Richard Sapir launch the story with a nice descriptive twist:

> *It was better than being in Afghanistan. In Afghanistan the bandits would shoot you from ambush, or if they captured you, they would cut you into pieces very slowly. Sometimes their women did it with their cooking tools.*
>
> *Sometimes the officers would throw you under the treads of a tank if they thought you might desert. Afghanistan was where you died horribly.*

We don't know where this fellow is, but he's seen worse. And, by implication, his present posting is no bed of roses, either.

In *Flight 741* (Gold Eagle, 1986), the scene is set for a traumatic skyjack when the routine movements of an airport cleaning crew are examined:

> *The weapons came aboard in Munich with the cleanup crew. Although security precautions in the terminal were stiff, no one detected their presence before they reached the plane. And for the personnel involved with terminal security, the members of the cleanup crew did not exist.*
>
> *The scrubbers went about their jobs unnoticed, unsupervised. Their uniforms and ID cards rendered them invisible, except in an emergency. If some unfortunate lost his breakfast on the concourse, or if the toilets overflowed, an urgent summons brought the men and women up "from maintenance," a kind of limbo somewhere out of sight and out of mind. But in the absence of a crisis, they were faceless and forgotten, worker ants who scoured the terminal and picked the*

grounded aircraft clean. If these cleaners had private lives and secret dreams, nobody paused to give the matter any thought.

Introducing Characters

If you employ your hook to introduce a character, you have two major angles of attack. A narrative approach is the more common, and you have your options: you can play God here, or let the character speak for himself, as Carroll Daly did in "Knights of the Open Palm":

> *Race Williams, Private Investigator, that's what the gilt letters spell across the door of my office. It don't mean nothing, but the police have been looking me over so much lately that I really need a place to receive them. You see I don't want them coming to my home; not that I'm overparticular, but a fellow must draw the line somewheres.*
>
> *As for my business, I'm what you might call a middleman — just a halfway house between the dicks and the crooks. Oh, there ain't no doubt that both the cops and crooks take me for a gun, but I ain't — not rightly speaking. I do a little honest shooting once in a while — just in the way of business.*

If you opt for third-person, as most action writers are prone to do these days, there are various ways for a character intro to kick off your story. You don't need descriptions, per se, but your hook ought to capture a character's *essence* as quickly as possible. Note how veteran Robert Daley sets up his heroine on the first page of *Hands of a Stranger* (Signet, 1985):

> *The first rape victim that morning was a nineteen-year-old black girl. The second was a thirty-eight-year-old white housewife. Assistant District Attorney Judith Adler could not do much for either.*

Shane Stevens, in *By Reason of Insanity* (Dell, 1979), leads off with a bizarre and chilling introduction to his villain, Thomas Bishop:

> *The flames ate at the body ravenously, searing, tearing through flesh and muscle. First flaking, then blackening and charring, the skin disintegrating swiftly. Soon arms, legs and trunk would become flame-*

flushed down to whitened bone. And in due time the head, stripped of facial features, would come to resemble a skull.

Silent now but for a gurgling singsong moan from somewhere deep in his throat, his eyes maniacal in the red glow of the fire, the boy watched his mother's body burn and burn and burn. . . .

You *know* that kid has problems, and the odds are fair that mama's death was not an accident. Before the author's done, we'll have an opportunity to watch his grim creation grow before our eyes, becoming one of the more frightening protagonists in recent fiction.

Mike McCray takes a different tack in *Contract: White Lady* (Dell, 1984), opening with his character in motion:

It took Beeker a block and a half to realize he was being followed. He knew it from the vague uneasiness in his gut—a gnawing feeling too faint to register. Anyone else would've ignored it. Anyone, that is, who hadn't survived five long years in the deadly jungles between Vietnam and Laos. One thing Beeker learned early in Nam: If you wanted to stay alive five senses weren't enough. The others were the ones that mattered—the ones most people weren't even aware of. If your gut says someone's following you, you damn well better listen. Beeker listened.

Again, as with the *Hill House* passage, we have edged into a capsule history without a lot of excess verbiage making it a painful exercise. We know that Beeker is a veteran of sorts, with more than average combat time, and if we had to we could probably approximate his age. We have an inkling of his skills, and now we share his knowledge that he's being followed— possibly by someone who may wish him harm—thus setting up the mood for confrontation.

William Nolan's introduction to a killer, in "A Real Nice Guy," approaches poetry in its simplicity and structure, but it tells us everything we need to know and hooks us in the bargain:

Warm sun.
A summer afternoon.
The sniper emerged from the roof door, walking easily, carrying a custom-leather guncase.

Opened the case.
Assembled the weapon.
Loaded it.
Sighted the street below.
Adjusted the focus.
Waited.
There was no hurry.
No hurry at all.

The gunman could be any age or race, a giant or a dwarf, but I would wager every reader of that opening can *see* him in the mind's eye, crystal clear. The structure of the sentences define his thoughts, meticulous and sharp, dissecting life with surgical precision. This is one bad dude, he's scary— and we can't afford to look away.

Eternal Triangle (Gold Eagle, 1987) opens with a rather different portrait of a villain, whose identity is not revealed until the book is more than half finished:

The basement bore a musty scent of long disuse. It was several days since he had ventured down into his secret place, and now the hunter flared his nostrils, picking out the separate, familiar smells of dust and mildew, age and slow decay. He knew what lay below. The darkness held no secrets from him; it inspired no apprehension in the hunter's heart or mind. The darkness was an old and trusted friend.

Another nifty way of using characters to bait your hook is via dialogue. With this technique, we eavesdrop on a private conversation, gleaning bits of information on the individuals, their problems, and their setting in the process.

The Trial (Gold Eagle, 1986) uses an opening with dialogue to introduce the heavies in the midst of plotting a conspiracy:

"You're sure it's gonna work?"
The rancher spent a moment firing up his fat cigar before he answered. The stogie lit, he blew a cloud of smoke toward the veranda ceiling. "I'm sure. If everybody does their part, it's in the bag."
"You better see they do their part."

The threat was thinly veiled, but the rancher ignored it, drawing deeply on the fine Havana leaf. His companion was obviously nervous, and it gave the rancher all the edge that he would ever need. "I've got it covered. Trust me."

The hook for *Time to Kill* (Gold Eagle, 1987) is ominous in different ways, but the same technique is employed to put the characters in place:

"C'mon, then, lass. It's nae much farther."

Rebecca Rafferty glanced back in the direction of Cairnaben, where the scattered lights looked warm and welcoming. Too far, she thought, but kept it to herself and reached for Tommy Cullen's hand. He helped her up the slope and led her toward the hulking shadow of the castle, still a hundred meters distant.

"Are you sure nobody's there?" she asked again.

"Of course I'm sure," he told her reassuringly. "The laird's gone inta Glasgow, as I told ye. D'ye think I'd bring ye up here for a public show?"

In *Run to Ground* (Gold Eagle, 1987), dialogue lulls the reader — and characters — into a fatal sense of false security:

"I'm getting too damned old for this."

"You're twenty-eight."

"That's too damned old."

And he was right. At twenty-eight, with six years on the job, Roy Jessup was already sick of staring at the border, waiting for the wets to make their way across by moonlight. He had not expected high adventure when he joined the Border Patrol straight out of college . . . not exactly. Still, there had been all those movies: Charlie Bronson, Kris Kristofferson, Jack Nicholson, all fighting major-league corruption in the desert sunshine, running up their score against the smugglers and top coyotes, but it only went to prove that life bore no relationship to Hollywood. With six long years in uniform, Roy Jessup had not seen a gram of coke outside of parties, never fired his gun in anger, never stumbled into an adventure ripe and waiting for a tough young stud to bring the house down.

"Hell, you're just a kid," his partner growled.

As seen in this example, openings with dialogue leave room for more traditional descriptive passages if they are handled carefully. One method need not necessarily exclude the other. Mix and match until you're comfortable with the results.

Enter Shooting

The favorite hook for many genre writers is an action scene with solid punch behind it, guaranteed to catch the reader's interest on page one. Immediate involvement is the prime advantage of an action opener, but there are other benefits as well. A hot beginning lets the writer pace himself, down-range, incorporating flashbacks to provide more background on his characters, their problems and relationships.

Don Pendleton did not invent the action hook, by any means, but he refined it to a modern art form in the early Bolan novels like *Chicago Wipeout* (Pinnacle, 1971):

> *In a matter of seconds, Bolan knew, the Chicago War would be on. The face in his crosshairs was the one he had been patiently waiting for for two hours on this crisp winter afternoon beside Lake Michigan. Faces had come and gone through the hairs of the 20-power, but this was the one he wanted. Once it might have been handsome, or at least it might have possessed a potential for comeliness. Now it showed the indelible tracings of an inner rot, of power and greed too long unrestrained—a face that had seen death and brutality and atrocity far too many times to remain comely in the mirror of humanity—and, yes, this was a face to launch the War for Chicago.*

In *Vegas Vendetta* (Pinnacle, 1971), we find the Executioner geared up for action in a desert wasteland:

> *The task was simple, and yet tinglingly complex. All he had to do was halt two powerful vehicles, overcome the natural resistance of at least ten heavily-armed Mafia gunners, liberate an awesome shipment of illicit gambling profits, and withdraw along a narrow route of retreat*

before the base camp reserves could get into the act.

And he had to do it in fifty seconds.

Pendleton establishes his story's mood by giving the hero a time limit, right up front. It's the equivalent of time bombs ticking down to Doomsday in the movies, and it works, unless it's overused.

If the moments prior to combat don't provide you with the necessary tension for a scene, you might consider picking up your story with the battle underway. In *Hatchet Man* (Warner Books, 1982), Dane Hartman brings the action home to San Francisco for a tour of the town with Dirty Harry Callahan:

> *By all rights, Jay Kuong Chien should have died with the rest of them. When the Japanese kid came into his uncle's store and pulled the VZ61 machine pistol out from under his coat, Jay should have been sitting on the stack of Chinese comic books next to the curtained door on the back wall. If he had, it was certain that he would have been killed with his uncle and the one store patron in the first sweep of the gun's ten 7.65mm bullets.*

Of course, Jay *isn't* killed, and thereby hangs the tale.

And while we're talking guns, it would be difficult to find a hook with greater impact than the one devised by William Nolan for "The White Cad Cross-Up":

> *The Marshal's big automatic crashed twice, and two .45 slugs whacked into my chest. At close range, the force of the bullets drove me back like a boxer's fists, and I landed on the rug, gasping and plenty nervous.*

Which, I suspect, may be the classic understatement of the decade.

Once upon a time, Gold Eagle's editors prepared a set of writer's guidelines for prospective members of the Bolan team, requiring that each book should open with the Executioner in action, squaring off against the enemy. This was the "Pendleton formula," demonstrably successful, but it soon proved too restrictive for a group of writers turning out a dozen books per year. The rule was scrapped, but there is still a great deal to be said for opening an action yarn with good old-fashioned *action*.

Anyway, it couldn't hurt.

The Lethal Cameo

I often like to lead with action scenes involving "throwaway" characters, whose death or close proximity to lethal violence will set the story rolling well before my hero shows his face. In *Rogue Force* (Gold Eagle, 1987), the novel opens with a military exercise as viewed from the perspective of a character with only moments left to live:

> *The night patrol had been a practice run, but it was turning into something else. The soldier had no fear of darkness, or the forest, but he didn't like the way his three companions had been acting. There had been none of the hilarity that usually accompanied their jungle milk runs, no suggestion that they ought to take it easy for an hour or two, then head on back to give their customary all-clear signal. Everybody knew the night patrols were basic drills that any trooper worth his salt had mastered long ago. The enemy was miles away—assuming that there was an enemy—and it would be a frosty day in hell before they got this far.*
>
> *He didn't mind the night patrols . . . until this one. All day long the others had been looking through him as if he wasn't there, responding to his questions curtly, if at all. He wondered whether he had unwittingly stepped on someone's toes, or if he had begun to snore in barracks after lights-out. Anything, make it anything, as long as no one knew.*

Another "throwaway" is used to bait the hook for an *Assault on Rome* (Gold Eagle, 1987):

> *The runner dared not pause for breath, although his lungs were burning, starved for oxygen as he raced through the musty catacombs. Behind him, death was closing rapidly, intent on running him to earth before he could escape.*
>
> *As if escape were possible.*

The same technique was also useful as a springboard for *The Fiery Cross* (Gold Eagle, 1988):

The young man stumbled, lost his stride and nearly fell. A sapling saved him, kept him on his feet, although the rough bark flayed his palms. The pain was nothing. Less than nothing. He had suffered worse, and he was running for his life.

Behind him, voices in the darkness. Cursing. Calling after him. Demanding that he stop and take his medicine. He could not hear the dogs yammering—not yet—but they were sometimes trained to hunt in silence, and they might be closing on him even now.

None of these characters survives for more than half a dozen pages, but their passing sets the stage for subsequent events and gives my hero something to investigate, avenge—whatever.

One-Liners

We've already stressed economy of language as a crucial part of writing decent hooks, and savvy authors sometimes take that concept to its logical conclusion. Several of the cleanest openings I've seen deliver all they need to in a single line.

The line can be simplicity itself, as in Douglas Fairbairn's brilliant novel, *Shoot*:

This is what happened.

Okay, and what more do we need? Stephen King liked Fairbairn's hook so much he lifted it, intact, to launch "The Mist," and I admire his choice. The terse one-liner puts us instantly in mind of tales around a campfire—or around a table in your favorite bar—and adds a ring of authenticity to everything that follows.

Short beginnings may appear innocuous, as in "The Dust," by Al Sarrantonio:

There was more of the dust.

Oh, really? Which dust is that, may we ask? And why, oh why, do we suspect immediately that we're dealing with a problem *so* much worse than shoddy housekeeping?

63

Simple hooks may pose a question, as in Stephen King's short work, "The Woman in the Room":

> *The question is: Can he do it?*

Do *what?* And, come to think of it, does anybody really need to ask?

Or they can pose a pretty problem, as in "The Body Politic," from Clive Barker:

> *Whenever he woke, Charlie George's hands stood still.*

Stretching our imaginations, William Nolan drops this bombshell at the opening of "Dead Call":

> *Len had been dead a month when the phone rang.*

And stretching still further, for Alan Ryan's "Onawa":

> *Yesterday—almost three hundred years ago now—I bit off the head of a bird.*

Perhaps the ultimate one-liner was delivered in *Killer*, the autobiography of a retired hit man known simply as "Joey":

> *Fuck* The Godfather.

I don't know about you, but he's got *my* attention, and if the subsequent chapters sound much like a tired rehash of *The Valachi Papers* . . . well, I'm almost ready to forgive him that. Because he baits a damn fine hook.

Back to the Future

Retrospective prologues used to be the rage in action series, filling in some background on the major characters and spelling out their "cause." The early *Executioners*, from Pinnacle, used retrospectives to acquaint new readers with the series and provide a sense of continuity. The method has its pros and cons; it can be repetitious—i.e., *boring*—for established fans, and there are other ways of sketching in your hero's past. With better than a hundred episodes in print, the publishers of Bolan novels have abandoned retrospective prologues as a formulaic waste of time and space that can be used to tell a brand-new story. Still, the method sometimes has a place in single titles like *Confessional*, *The Choirboys*, *Triangle*, and *Child of Blood*.

Reeling In the Catch

Your story, to a large extent, should dictate the selection of a hook. If you concern yourself with cops and robbers, you may want to open with the crime. A private eye? Why not an introduction to his latest client, or some incident that will compel him to accept a deadly case? If you are comfortable with counter-terrorism, you may wish to open from the viewpoint of your villains, plotting dastardly conspiracies and thereby setting up your hero's entrance in a later scene. If all else fails, there is that tested standby: the assassination of a victim who turns out to be the hero's partner/lover/brother/closest friend from college or the army . . . well, you get the drift. Mechanics of the murder set your story rolling, and the hook will leave a host of questions to be answered by your hero, somewhere down the line.

With all of this in mind, what sort of opening should you employ?

Remember that the hook should be the springboard for your novel, launching readers into an adventure they won't soon forget (you hope). If your springboard doesn't give the readers adequate velocity, they fall short of your story, interest-wise. You'll recognize the feeling, if you've ever tried a diving board so stiff it bruised your feet and knocked you off your stride. A painful belly-flop is the result, in either case.

It's not enough to bait a flashy hook, however. Come what may, you have to reel in your catch—the readers—and make delivery on your promise of a story worth their time (and money). In the short run, you may con your audience with sound and fury, signifying nothing, but the dullest fan will have your number soon, and ripped-off readers won't be coming back. Intimidated? Don't be. Just remember that you're not alone out there. You've got an army on your side—your characters—and they'll do anything you say to keep the story moving briskly. All you have to do is give them life and tell them where to go. The rest is easy . . . more or less.

6. Lights . . . Camera . . . Action!

We have established that an action yarn must hook its readers early on, if it has any reasonable chance of being a success. Long paragraphs (or *pages*, God forbid!) of exposition simply will not cut the mustard here. You don't need smoking pistols or a bloodbath, necessarily, and your protagonist need not appear, but if you spend the first half chapter setting up a peaceful scene, your readers may not stick around to find out what comes next.

At this point, I should mention that it's not enough to open strong and finish with a stack of bodies. In between the hook and the final showdown lies your story, and your audience is looking for adventure all the way. They won't be satisfied with one or two quick fixes buried in a boring travelogue. If you propose to deal in action and adventure, you must be prepared to make delivery on both.

Adventure, Anyone?

For openers, we must agree on definitions. Checking out my trusty dictionary, I perceive that *action* is "the state of being active." Simple, right? Each time you walk across a room or eat a sandwich you are taking part in action, of a sort. *Adventure*, on the other hand, confines our scrutiny to actions that involve "a risk, unforseeable danger, or unexpected excitement; an exciting or remarkable experience." Selecting groceries in the supermarket is an action, but unless you suffer from agoraphobia, it hardly qualifies as an adventure. Likewise, urban freeways are a nonstop cavalcade of motion, but I dare say most of us can watch the cars go by all day without discovering a plot that holds our interest.

We've established that adventure stories are, in essence, modernized heroic quests. Through plotting, you determine where the characters are going, how they get there (if they get there), and the ultimate success or failure of their efforts. Action, in this context, is designed to serve your plot and the development (or the degeneration) of your characters. To some extent, you must eliminate the non-essentials — showers, visits to the rest room, meals and haircuts — in a bid to keep your story streamlined, moving with deliberate purpose.

I am not suggesting that a novel should contain *no* action that diverges from the central story line. The "Dirty Harry" movies are a perfect case in point: Throughout each story, the protagonist is briefly and dramatically distracted from his quest to cope with robbers, terrorists, and sundry other misfits. His response to different confrontations serves a purpose by establishing his character through *action*, leaving viewers in no doubt about the kind of hero they are dealing with. When Harry is allowed to go about his business, tracking down the major villain of the piece, we know precisely what that villain may expect as his reward.

Conversely, interruptions in the story line that merely serve as padding may be detrimental to your work, regardless of the action they contain. Be careful with digressions, using them to help develop characters or build suspense; remember that if they serve no useful purpose, you are simply wasting time.

As mentioned earlier, an outline may be helpful as you work to keep your plot on track. By jotting down your thoughts and stray scenarios as they suggest themselves, arranging them in some approximation of their final order, you may notice gaping loopholes in the plot . . . or find your favorite scene to be expendable. The *story* must take precedence above all else, and it should not be twisted out of shape to justify inclusion of a "catchy" episode. If you're primarily concerned about the fact that no one has been killed or bedded in the past two chapters, I suggest that your priorities are out of whack.

The Quest

The way in which your characters proceed depends upon the characters themselves and on the nature of their quest. Pursuit of secret information may require more technical finesse than the construction of a plot to get revenge against an enemy. If loved ones are in jeopardy, your hero may proceed with greater care than if he merely stands to lose his job, his reputation, or a suitcase full of cash. Again, it all depends upon the man— or woman—and his personal reaction to the given situation. Some men, asked to choose between a million dollars and their wives, will take the money every time.

An action yarn, by definition, squares your hero off against a dangerous antagonist. The adversary need not be another human being—witness *Jaws* or *Alien*—nor must it necessarily be animate, if we are dealing with a force of nature, as in *Icefire* or *The Towering Inferno*. Any way you slice them, adversaries are the driving force behind adventure fiction; they provide the necessary conflict, place your hero in a situation where his jeopardy becomes intolerable and he is compelled to take decisive action. Your adventure lies within that jeopardy, the element of risk that he (or she) may not succeed in neutralizing the impending threat.

Antagonists may be conveniently divided into two main categories: they are either known or unknown to your hero. There is never any doubt about the enemy's identity in *Jaws*, the James Bond novels, or the early Bolan series. Jeopardy arises from the question of our hero's personal ability to cope with lethal adversaries. How will good Chief Brody find the killer shark in time to save his job, his marriage, and his town? Can one intrepid warrior stand alone against the Mafia, the KGB, or SPECTRE? Readers may *presume* the hero will prevail, but they can never know for sure until they read the final page, and therein lies adventure.

On the flipside, unknown adversaries mingle mystery and action in a bid to keep the hero and the reader guessing to the point of climax, when the masks are dropped and traitors are exposed to cleansing daylight. Robert Ludlum takes the honors here, with layers of double-, triple-, and quadruple-cross so intricately woven through the fabric of his stories that his readers—like a Ludlum hero—can't trust *anyone*.

A character's response to different challenges will necessarily depend upon the nature of his adversaries. If the enemy is known, your story may amount to a straightforward chase, climaxed when your hero overtakes his quarry—or, in the alternative, is himself forced to stand and fight. Conversely, if the enemy's identity is secret, the protagonist will have to search for vital clues, perhaps enduring attacks to lure his adversary out of hiding for the final showdown. Why has dynamite been wired to the ignition of your hero's car? Who fired that bullet through his bedroom window late at night? Is that a man's voice, or a woman's, on the telephone? Who abducted your hero's lover — the CIA, the KGB, or just an "ordinary" psychopath?

Remember, in constructing the reaction of protagonists to high-risk situations, that a character works best when he or she remains *in* character. A radical departure from established personality must be explained and justified before your editors and readers will accept the change. You can't expect Paul Kersey, in the *Death Wish* series, to sit idly by and watch while muggers victimize a woman on the subway. Likewise, Pee Wee Herman probably would not produce a .38 and mow the scumbags down if situations were reversed. Unless you're dealing with a maniac, there should be logic in the actions of your characters, and timid souls will not respond with force unless they are compelled by overwhelming circumstances, as with Farrah Fawcett in *Extremities* or Dustin Hoffman's wimpy character in *Straw Dogs*. Keep your people true-to-life, and they should serve you well.

Believability

Setting up an action scene within a novel makes demands upon an author's eye for detail, capacity for research, imagination, and ability to edit final copy. Ideal action sequences are both exciting and informative; they spike the reader's pulse and keep the story moving, all at once. Like women's skirts, they should be long enough to cover the subject and short enough to be interesting.

That said, what *is* an action scene? Within the definition of the modern genre, action sequences are those involving conflict, physical in nature, that provide your major characters with space in which to strut their stuff. The hero and his chief antagonist may not appear together every time — in fact, it gets old in a hurry if they *do* — but one side or the other will be pulling out the stops in an attempt to capture, kill, or otherwise distress the opposition.

Action scenes may run their course within a single paragraph, or they may be protracted over several chapters. Let your story be the guide, whenever possible, but bear in mind that needless padding slows things down and undermines suspense. Your hero may be threatened by a sniper on a crowded street, but do you really need *three* snipers? Half a dozen? Should he be pursued for miles on end, through heavy traffic, merely so that you can raise your word-count with a long description of the chase? (If you've been answering these questions with a cheerful yes, please reconsider at your earliest convenience. Like, right now.)

Successful action writers have a handle both on what to say and what is better left unsaid. We'll deal with graphic violence later; at the moment, I'm discussing style. In general, when preparing action sequences, I'd be inclined to say that "less is more," but you can also take the maxim to extremes and leave a scene devoid of substance, as in this example:

> Hickock faced the seven outlaws. At a signal, guns were drawn, and moments later Hickock stood alone.

They don't come any shorter, but where action is concerned, this "scene" possesses all the interest of a plot synopsis clipped from *TV Guide*. It's well and good to let readers exercise their own imagination, but your audience is paying you for entertainment here. That's where the verbs and adjectives come in. If Hickock is about to gun down seven men, your readers want to *see* it, in their mind's eye, and experience the smell of gunsmoke for themselves.

These days, we're told that millions of Americans would rather watch the tube or hit their local theater than read books. I tackle action sequences the other way around, by "watching" them before I put the words on paper.

How's that, again? He *watches* them?

That's right. In simple terms, I run a private "movie" in my own imagination. All my characters are present and accounted for — I'd recognize them anywhere — and I can put them through their paces any way I choose. Sometimes, I run the action in slow motion, like the final shootout from *The Wild Bunch*, watching people scatter, falling when they're hit, returning fire despite their wounds. It may take practice, but I dare say everyone has daydreamed in their time, and writers do it more than most. In fact, unless I'm very much preoccupied, I seldom look at any piece of scenery without imagining an action scene in progress, and I'm willing to lay odds that every fiction writer has a touch of Walter Mitty in his soul.

In order to provide the necessary punch, an action sequence must possess intrinsic credibility. The various components — setting, characters, and action — should be scrutinized in detail for mistakes and inconsistencies before you put a manuscript to bed. A careful editor may ferret out mistakes you've overlooked, but if it gets to be a habit, you'll be looking at rejection slips instead of royalty checks.

We'll have a great deal more to say about your characters in time, but here I must reemphasize the need for logic, credibility, and reason. If you know your people inside out, the way you should, you will be able to predict which ones are likely to be forceful, violent, cowardly, or stoic in the face of danger. "A" might no more leave his gun at home than he would leave his trousers; "B", conversely may absorb ferocious punishment without a whimper, praying for a hero who will save his bacon. Either way, your characters should logically behave as you have led your readers to expect in any given situation—or you should provide a reason for their sudden change of heart.

Unless you make a special point of "writing what you know," the setting for an action sequence may require some homework. On-site visits may not always be within your means—how many of us can afford to hit Karachi or Jakarta for the weekend?—but resorting to detailed maps and guidebooks may assist you. Once again, be careful; try to make your work precise. I once received a query from an editor about a car chase in Los Angeles: unconsciously, I had my heavies driving north, along a southbound one-way street!

Some authors, in the mold of Elmore Leonard, visit cities where their stories will be set and walk along the streets their characters will travel, stopping in to give the local bars and restaurants a try. I've talked to others who (supposedly) play out their action scenes by crawling through the shrubs at home and calculating fields of fire firsthand. A word of caution, here: Make sure you have a modicum of privacy before you start performing like a poor man's Rambo. Public escapades may prove embarrassing, to say the least.

The quest for credibility encompasses all aspects of an action scene. Your hero will become a butt of ridicule if he insists on leaping out of seventh-story windows onto handy awnings. Submachine guns firing at a cyclic rate of 750 rounds per minute will not hold the enemy at bay for hours with a single magazine of thirty cartridges. (And if your gunner's packing extras, keep the weight in mind; a dozen loaded magazines inserted in his pockets makes for one hellacious case of droopy drawers.) A tire iron cracked across your hero's unprotected skull will not result in "just a headache." Even Smokey and the Bandit had to stop for gas.

There are no ironclad rules about the "where" and "when" of action scenes within a manuscript. The action may take everyone (except the author!) by surprise: a bomb blast in the middle of a dinner party; an abduction or a drive-by shooting on a quiet residential street; an airplane's crashing through the roof of a hotel. Other scenes—especially climactic showdowns—may be telegraphed from the beginning, while a series of preliminary bouts maintain suspense. We *know* the hero has to meet his adversary in the end, but if the author knows his business, getting there is half the fun.

Your story primes the pump for action scenes, and so it dictates their construction. No one can advise you on the type of gun a character should carry in his belt, the make of car he ought to drive, his brand of cigarettes, or other such minutiae. Beware of slavish imitation—hard-boiled cops who violate department regulations by their choice of handguns are a prime example—and remember that suspense must have a solid foothold in reality.

While we're discussing credibility, it is an excellent idea to take some notes as you complete an action scene. How many shots were fired? Who bit the big one? If a crucial character is wounded, make a note of his condition in the interest of consistency. (When Dr. Watson first meets Sherlock Holmes, we learn about his recent shoulder wound, sustained while serving with the army in Afghanistan; a few adventures down the road, we find the doctor limping from his old *leg* wound.) When Dirty Harry loses track of bullets fired in anger, you can bet he's playing games, but it can be embarrassing when characters return, unbidden, from the dead.

Pacing

As you prepare your outline, keep in mind the necessary elements of a successful action plot. The first of these—and the most difficult for many fledgling writers to control—is *pacing*. Action/adventure novels must, by definition, have action, but please bear in mind that nobody fights and fornicates *all* the time. (Even Hell's Angels take naps now and then!) You normally won't show your characters consuming every meal or making visits to the restroom, but you should allow for normal functions like fatigue and rest, confusion, indecision, strategy discussions, and the like. In comic books, you may have only six or seven pages to complete your story, but we're working on a novel here. Relax and take your time.

Successful pacing is achieved by breaking up the action at strategic points, allowing readers — and your characters — to take a breather now and then. Your people will look silly if they simply race from one brawl to another, piling up a massive body-count at the expense of common sense. Remember that your characters are human, even though you made them up, and show them some consideration. After all, their *lives* are on the line.

Intrusion on the mainstream narrative must be accomplished skillfully, and there are several ways to pull it off. The *flashback*, properly employed, can be a useful tool, providing the author with a chance to call "time-out" while filling in some background on a crucial person, place, or problem. In *Red Dragon*, Thomas Harris interrupts the driving action for three chapters to fill in the past of his awesome monster, Francis Dolarhyde. I used a similar technique in *Child of Blood*, employing flashbacks to flesh out each major character as their lives converged on a collision course. It works — but, I should add, it can become a hopeless mess if you are simply rambling, killing time.

Another useful weapon in your arsenal is that old movie stand-by, *change of scene*. Your hero's getting tired from hot pursuit in three straight chapters? Never fear. Let's give the guy (or gal) a break, and look around for someone else to play with. If your leading man is hiding out from mobsters or preparing to annihilate the Sandinistas, what's his girlfriend doing? Is she thinking of him? Looking for him? Getting into trouble on her own? And what about the heavies? Are they conscious of the danger closing on their flank? Are they pursuing Mr. Clean? Inquiring minds want to know.

The passage of time in a story is up to the author. A novel's action may span hours or centuries, depending on the story and the writer's natural ability to pull it off. The premiere *Executioner* encompassed two full months in something like 180 pages; most, since then, have limited their action to a period of days, to keep the hero hopping. Generally, more time means more deletions of material, in terms of trivial activities like eating, sleeping, warming up the family car, and so forth. You are not required to catalogue each movement made by every character throughout a given day. It's boring, dig it?

And within the action genre, boring readers is a capital offense.

Tension and Suspense

A second necessary element of plotting, *tension*, is connected inextricably with pacing. It arises naturally — or *should* — from complications your characters confront en route to the solution of a problem. Bear in mind, however, that if your protagonist is constantly in danger, if he never gets a break and his potential risks become a matter of routine, your story may begin to plod. (Check out your average, bargain-basement slasher movie, if you still have doubts. Assuming you can stay awake, you'll notice how the carbon-copy "shocks" and "frights" all start to look alike as time goes by. If you've seen one guy jump out of a closet shouting "Boo!" you've seen them all.)

There are varieties of tension, and they don't all hinge upon a threat to life or limb. There may be tension in the interaction of your characters, beyond the root antagonisms of the story. Are they basically suspicious of each other, even though they seem to share a common goal? Have the adherents of two disparate religions or political beliefs been thrown together by a twist of circumstance? Is hero "A" attracted physically to lady "B", and does she share his feelings, even though she cannot bring herself to let it show?

Effective tension may be found within a single character, if we take time to look. Is your protagonist an alcoholic, terrified of falling off the wagon in the middle of his biggest mission ever? Is he sweating out results of diagnostic tests from his physician? Is his job in jeopardy from something he may be forced to do? Is your protagonist the victim of a phobia, compelled to overcome private demons in a bid to save loved ones?

In *The Liquidator*, Boise Oakes is an assassin who has never murdered anybody in his life. Selected for the job capriciously, he carries on by farming out official contracts to a hit man, but, inevitably, he is forced to take the field alone. Will Graham, in *Red Dragon*, is a federal agent with a knack for tracking human monsters. He can "get inside" their twisted minds, by methods even he does not completely understand, and he is terrified when one of them suggests that he and those he stalks are "just alike." In *Child of Blood*, with Tony Kieu, I drew the portrait of a boy whose longing for a family is overshadowed by his hatred for the father who abandoned him in Vietnam. Instead of reaching out for love, he is compelled to kill.

We're looking at the heart and soul of all adventure fiction, and the sad truth is that many working authors *still* don't get it. One man running endlessly around a track is active, but there's no adventure to it. No *suspense*. You need at least two runners, giving everything they've got in competition, striving for the finish line, before you have a race. And waiting for the outcome, cheering on our favorite athlete, we experience suspense.

Remembering the standard definition of adventure, authors in the genre should invest their stories with the necessary elements of danger, risk, excitement, and surprise. I wouldn't try to serve them up the same way every time, by any means, but if you're working on a story that has none of the above, it's simply not adventure. Sorry.

There are probably as many ways to build suspense as there are authors working in the field. Again, there are no magic guidelines for construction of a good, suspenseful scene, but with some practice, you should find a way to build on the established methods used by other pros. And, who can say? You might come up with something new.

In order to create suspense, your characters must obviously face some kind of jeopardy. A threat to life and limb will normally evolve at some point in the story, but it doesn't have to start that way. In *Mr. Majestyk*, the title character is first threatened economically, by corrupt labor contractors, faced with the possible loss of his melon crop. Murder comes later, when he has resisted the opening moves of his enemies, building a mood of suspense as the jeopardy escalates.

Suspense may have little or nothing to do with your story's eventual outcome. We all know that Charles DeGaulle died of old age, but *Day of the Jackal* is still a suspense masterpiece, following his would-be assassin down the tortuous path to ultimate failure. Likewise, the protagonist in *D.O.A.* has only hours to live; there is no magic antidote to save him from the poison he's ingested, but we're rooting for him all the same, as he attempts to track down his killer before his time runs out. Series fans are confident their hero will survive, but they are interested in *how* he does it in the face of overwhelming odds.

Suspense.

One tried-and-true technique of building up the mood is through foreshadowing. A skillful author lays the groundwork for a crisis situation by providing clues along the way: a chance remark, or something left unsaid; a pointed glance; the hero's vague suspicion that he's being followed. (Not-so-skillful authors use this method, too; they just don't do it very well.)

It's not enough for you to know that trouble's on the way; your readers should be able to deduce as much from indications in the story. If they can't, they won't be hanging on the edges of their seats to see what happens next. They'll merely be surprised . . . assuming that they haven't moved along, by then, to a more entertaining tale.

Foreshadowing is frequently accomplished by insertion of mysterious, unexplained incidents throughout the story. A nondescript sedan follows our hero through midtown traffic, turning up outside his home by night. A lovely woman passes him a cryptic note while riding on the subway — and immediately disappears. An apartment is ransacked, but nothing appears to be missing. The protagonist's wife/lover/best friend/business partner vanishes without a trace. (Please bear in mind that all your clues must be explained by the conclusion of the story; otherwise, they just become embarrassing loose ends.)

Suspense within an action scene derives from choreography. It's more than dodging bullets in a firefight or evading hot pursuit, however. Once the action's been engaged, remember that you can't rely on twenty-five near-misses in a row to keep things moving. Even sudden death gets boring, if it always looks the same.

Remember that your action scenes can be described from different points of view. We may be looking through the hero's eyes as he ascends a flight of stairs, expecting an attack at any moment. When it comes, you might shift to the heavy's perspective and learn how it feels to attack from the darkness, ferociously slashing away at your nemesis. Take that as far as it goes, then return to your primary viewpoint as "A" starts to fight for his life. If the action involves several characters, so much the better. They each have a viewpoint and feelings, remember. Why else are they there?

You need not carry each and every action scene to an explicit climax. Action may be interrupted, in the interest of suspense, as when the villain closes Chapter 3 by whipping out his gun but doesn't get to fire until the start of Chapter 5. Some other sequences may *never* be completed. When a psycho-killer locks the door behind his next intended victim and begins to smile, we know what's on his mind. The subsequent discovery of a body or an empty, vandalized apartment may be all we need to make the scene complete. It isn't blazing action, necessarily, but it's effective if you handle it correctly. With a bit of luck, imagination does the rest.

If you've paced yourself correctly, keeping all your goals in mind, the climax of your story should become its hottest action scene. It may not be a battle fielding armies; you can stage a one-on-one between your hero and his leading adversary just as well. Remember, as you plan the final scene, that readers have been rooting for your hero since page one, or thereabouts. They want to see him win, but no one likes the title bout to wind up as a one-punch knockout. Likewise, if the audience has come to hate your villain, they don't want him getting off the hook *too* easily.

That doesn't mean you have to shoot him six or seven times; he simply needs an opportunity to die with style. Or, maybe not. A sampling of the daily news reminds us that the bad guys often get away—one-quarter of domestic murders go unsolved each year—and you may wish to leave the ending of your story flexible, as in the novel *Road Kills*. There, a vicious serial slayer disappears on Florida's Alligator Alley, presumably winding up as 'gator bait. "Or maybe," the author suggests, "some damned fool gave him a ride."

A final classic flaw sometimes emerges when an author strives too hard for final-page suspense and thereby blows his chance to make a good, clean kill. If you're familiar with the television series "Batman," you'll recall the famous cliff-hanger scenes, invariably closing for the day with Batman and Robin attached to some Rube Goldberg device, intended to kill them slowly while the heavies make a leisurely escape. The problem was that no one ever stayed behind to verify the kill, and everyone (except the "brilliant" villains) knew that Batman would escape with seconds left to spare. This kind of ending works occasionally, as when James Bond runs a vicious gauntlet at the end of *Dr. No*, but it becomes a joke if overused.

With all of the above in mind, it's time to meet the people who will make your story come to life. I think you'll find that some of them may look familiar. They've been with you all along.

7. Heroes and Heavies

Picture a deserted city. Streets are empty, shops and houses uninhabited. There is no sign of life, no sound. The very atmosphere is dusty, dead. You have to concentrate on breathing, and you get the feeling that a spoken word will shrivel up and die of loneliness before it leaves your lips.

A ghost town makes the perfect introduction for a mystery . . . but let's suppose the streets remain deserted, silent. No one *ever* comes on stage. From an intriguing hook, you've plummeted to instant tedium. You're looking at an Andy Warhol snoozer, guaranteed.

In short, until you populate the scenery, you've got no story. *How* you populate your fiction may determine whether you succeed as a professional or simply fade away with all the other hapless "wanna-bees." Your characters can make or break a novel at the outset. Bring them vividly to life, for good or evil, and the best (or worst) of them can help you elevate a mediocre plot above its origins. Conversely, if you try to muddle through with cardboard characters, the greatest story in the world may come off sounding like a retread of the Hardy Boys.

Okay, I grant you, everybody knows you're dreaming up these characters, but they should still seem real, imbued with spirit, individuality, and style. Your readers want them to be real—or realistic, anyway—and it's your job, as author and creator, to fulfill that wish. Before we're finished, you should have a handle on the process of creating "life" on paper, and from there, it's up to you.

If you've been faithful with your homework, namely reading anything and everything that you can get your hands on, you will recognize the fact that some professionals possess more skill than others when it comes to the creation of their characters. A few are gifted artists, sketching characters in bold, imaginative strokes, injecting subtle colors to complete the portrait, bringing it to life. The rank and file are capable enough, like good mechanics; everything they put together works all right, but sometimes we can still see nuts and bolts exposed. Too many labor on like cut-rate Frankensteins, well-meaning but inept, producing clumsy monsters that inevitably turn upon their masters, trashing their careers.

The cut-rate Frankensteins are also known as "hacks." Some still get work, at bargain-basement rates, but no one takes their product seriously. As a group and individually, they're going nowhere fast.

For openers, we need to look beyond the trivia of good and evil, race and sex, to understand that there are basically two kinds of characters in modern fiction: some that work, and some that don't. Don Pendleton once briefed me on the crucial difference, with a description of "created" versus "made-up" characters, and while the terminology is flexible, Don's choice of labels neatly pins down the problem.

Created characters, in simple terms, are those who have been "brought to life," invested by their authors with the many traits of human personality that make them seem to live and breathe. By contrast, *made-up* characters are lifeless, two-dimensional clichés, whipped up on impulse by a lazy writer in the same way faceless extras are employed by film directors, to produce a body-count. You never really get to know a made-up character, but it's a safe bet that you haven't missed a thing.

In Chapter 5, I mentioned "throwaways," the sort of characters who generally die by violence shortly after their appearance in a novel. They are used, most often, to provide your major characters with cannon fodder as the story rolls along, progressing toward its climax. As a rule of thumb, development of throwaways, as "living" characters, should be proportionate to the amount of time they spend on stage. If Mr. X is nothing but a target in your villain's shooting gallery, you may dismiss him with a line or two and go about your business. If, however, you expect your readers to feel sympathy—or *anything*—for Mr. X along the way, you'll have to spend a bit more time developing his character before you kill him off.

Profiles and Descriptions

I like to have my people ready by the time I finish polishing an outline. Characters will normally suggest themselves as I begin to lay out a story— they *are* the story, after all—and I write profiles on the major actors as I go along. Before I try to make them walk and talk, or kiss and kill, I want to know these people inside-out, their likes and dislikes, quirks and kinky habits—all the things that separate a person from his peers.

My profiles range in length from one or two short lines to half a page or more, depending on a character's importance to the story. They will normally include a detailed physical description, habits, sexual proclivities, political persuasions, taste in cars and clothing: anything, in short, that I can think of at the time. I end up writing down a great deal more than I will ever use, from moles and scars to ancient childhood traumas, but I need it all, and more, if I intend to build a living, breathing character from scratch.

The little things bring characters to life and make them memorable for your readers. Browse through Ian Fleming's work, and notice how he "signed" his characters with quirks and traits that make each one unique. Ernst Blofeld's lobeless ears and nostrils scarred by syphilis. Scaramanga's third nipple. Honeychile Rider's broken nose. The lethal hit man with a wart, in *Diamonds Are Forever*. (I forget his name, but I remember *him*, and what a brute he was.)

In short, the skillful use of trivia *can* make a difference. Anyone who reads your profiles should be able to identify your people if they put on solid flesh and walked into the room, but you should not go overboard and lose your story line in the pursuit of tasty odds and ends.

How much of a description is *too* much? Again, I'd say you ought to let the story be your guide. Don't feel compelled to give us every scar or liver spot on each and every character. Remember that your readers have imaginations, too, and half the fun of reading genre fiction lies in putting faces with the people, making each one *personal*. You'll recognize the feeling, if you've ever loved a novel and been blown away by sorry casting of a movie made for same. Imagine Don Knotts as James Bond . . . but, please, not while you're eating.

Some examples may be helpful in defining the parameters of adequate descriptions. For a start, meet Butt Cut Cates, as lovingly described by William Bradford Huie in *The Klansman*:

> Butt Cut's nickname was common in a county where the princi-
> pal occupation was the growing and processing of pine trees, either for
> lumber or pulpwood. "Butt cut" means massive might close to the
> ground. The first log cut from the base of a felled tree—the butt cut—

81

is the more massive, more noted for circumference than length. Twenty-nine years old, Butt Cut Cates was five-feet-six and weighed one-ninety. He was a human bulldozer. From the day he dropped out of the seventh grade until he was twenty-five he drove a pulpwood truck and learned "every pig trail in Atoka County." This knowledge of terrain was one of the reasons why Big Track, in 1962, made him his only deputy.

In *Black Sunday*, Thomas Harris introduces an Arab terrorist thus:

> Hafez Najeer, head of Al Fatah's elite Jihaz al-Rasd (RASD) field intelligence unit, sat at a desk leaning his head back against the wall. He was a tall man with a small head. His subordinates secretly called him "The Praying Mantis." To hold his full attention was to feel sick and frightened.
>
> Najeer was the commander of Black September. He did not believe in the concept of a "Middle East situation." The restoration of Palestine to the Arabs would not have elated him. He believed in holocaust, the fire that purifies.

Dashiell Hammett takes a different approach to the description of a character in "Too Many Have Lived":

> The man's tie was as orange as a sunset. He was a large man, tall and meaty, without softness. The dark hair parted in the middle, flattened to his scalp, his firm, full cheeks, the clothes that fit him with noticeable snugness, even the small pink ears flat against the sides of his head—each of these seemed but a differently colored part of one same, smooth surface. His age could have been thirty-five or forty-five.

Contrast Hammett's detailed description with the spare—but fully adequate—offering presented by Rex Stout in "Bullet for One":

> It was her complexion that made it hard to believe she was as scared as she said she was.

In *Houston Attack*, Carl Ramm pays more attention to the damsel in distress:

She had one of those ageless Mayan faces. High cheek-bones. Nut-colored skin. Onyx-black hair that hung down over the surprisingly ripe bosom swell. Hawker guessed her to be about eighteen, though she could have been thirty just as easily. But Indio women tend to get chubby and domestic when they hit their mid-twenties, and there was nothing chubby about this one. She was long and lithe, and Hawker could see that she had been crying.

For those who like a taste of metaphysics with their pulchritude, Dean Koontz offers this passage from *Twilight Eyes*:

She was wearing brown corduroy jeans and a brown-and-red-checkered blouse, and I vaguely noticed that her body was lean and excitingly proportioned, but truthfully I did not pay much attention to the way she was built — not then, later — for initially my attention was entirely captured by her hair and face. Thick, soft, silky, shimmering hair, too blond to be called auburn, too auburn to be blond, was combed across one side of her face, half obscuring one eye, reminding me of Veronica Lake, that movie star of an earlier era. If there was any fault at all in her exquisite face, it was that the very perfection of her features also gave her a slightly cool, distant, and unattainable look. Her eyes were large, blue, and limpid. The hot August sun streamed over her as if she were on a stage instead of perched on a battered wooden stool, and it didn't illuminate her the same way it did everyone else on the midway; the sun seemed to favor her, beaming upon her the way a father might look upon a favorite daughter, accenting the natural luster of her hair, proudly revealing the porcelain smoothness of her complexion, lovingly molding itself to her sculpted cheekbones and artfully chiseled nose, suggesting but not fully illuminating great depth and many mysteries in her entrancing eyes.

I think you get the drift. A *bad* description usually fails in one of two directions, either offering the reader so much useless detail that the mind clicks off, or shooting for the opposite approach with characters who come out vague and two dimensional. A cumbersome description stalls your readers in the middle of a story, while the other, nonexistent kind may leave them wondering who your people are, and why they act the way they do. (The worst I ever read, bar none, described two Puerto Rican terrorists as "small brown men full of hair." And what the hell does *that* mean?)

Imitating Life

Certain authors like to pattern major characters on real-life people, and they often choose celebrities. Don Pendleton once told me that he visualized Mack Bolan as a cross between Clint Eastwood and Clint Walker, but he also had the good sense *not* to say so in his novels. Mark Roberts, on the other hand, prefers to plumb the depths of propaganda in his *Soldier for Hire* series, using "Senator Ned Flannery" as an obvious stand-in for Ted Kennedy, branding his target an "idiot," "king of the sewer rats," and so forth.

There are certain perils to employing real-life models for your characters. If you become too obvious, you run the risk of libel suits from individuals who may resent depiction in your writing as a liberal-leftist-commie-scumbag. Such lawsuits are not common, but they happen, and the same risks may apply for authors who habitually plant the names of real-life friends (or enemies) within their work. More, later, on the name game. For the moment, let's just say that while "John Smith" is fairly safe, your next-door neighbor, Hubert Finkleheimer, may not wish to turn up in the bookstore as a child-molesting lunatic. (I can't imagine *why* he'd mind, but there you have it.)

A more common problem, in the use of obvious celebrity descriptions, is the risk of characters becoming "obsolete" with time. A classic case is that of Ian Fleming, who compared James Bond to Hoagy Carmichael in early novels of the series. That was fine in 1954, but it was wearing thin a decade later, when Sean Connery became James Bond for countless moviegoers. I suspect the general reaction from a crop of younger readers, picking up a Fleming novel in the nineties, will be "Hoagy *Who?*"

Above all else, celebrity descriptions carved in stone — or etched on paper — may deprive your readers of the major kick they get from reading action novels: namely, using the imagination to identify themselves with favorite characters. Suppose your fans don't care for Charlie Bronson's mustache, Ernest Borgnine's ample gut — whatever? If you absolutely *must* relate your character descriptions to celebrities, be circumspect. Don't do it *all* the time, and try your best to ditch this shopworn crutch as soon as possible. Remember that you're writing fiction here, not casting for the silver screen.

A Question of Motive

With all of that in mind, you'll find the physical description of your characters to be the easy part. Determining their *motivations* is a far more complicated task—and one you must not neglect, if you intend to deal with memorable, lifelike characters.

Each voluntary move we make, throughout the day, is executed for a reason. That is not to say our motives are invariably rational, or even conscious, but they still exist. There is a world of difference between the motives of, let's say, an Albert Schweitzer and a Jack the Ripper, but they both had reasons for behaving in the ways that made them famous. Altruistic, generous, or sick and twisted, motivations come in every color of the psychic rainbow, and you ought to be on speaking terms with all of them. Your characters may not be fully conscious of their motivation all the time, but *you*, as their creator, must be. If you don't know what they're doing, there's no way on earth to make them do it well.

The motivation of a character may be revealed in several ways. Most common of the lot is simple exposition, in which you, the narrator, sit down and tell the reader how your people think and feel. A fair example is my introduction to Mack Bolan, incorporated by Don Pendleton in *The Executioner's War Book* (Pinnacle, 1977):

> Bolan's ability to kill in cold blood indicated no lack of emotion or commitment in the man himself. If anything, Mack Bolan might be described as a purist, even an idealist, with deeply held convictions concerning the nature of good and evil. Unwilling to compromise the basic principles learned in childhood, Bolan found no need to feign embarrassment over the fundamental concepts of morality and patriotism. His choice of the military as a career was therefore natural, and his selfless dedication to the opposition of Communist aggression in Asia personally unavoidable. It was not for Bolan to delegate the defense of basic freedom to others.

In *Paramilitary Plot* (Gold Eagle, 1982), we get a look inside a different kind of soldier:

> The memory of his Asian wars stirred mixed feelings in the colonel. It was like they said: the best and worst of times. Nam had been a

85

new awakening for Rosky, the peak—and demise—of his career as a
regular soldier. He had taken to the jungle like a duck to water, knowing
that this war was what he had spent his youth in preparation for. Viet-
nam provided Rosky with a sense of purpose, a focus. It made him
whole.

And he was good at what he did—maybe the best. His success
had caused embarrassment to other less aggressive field commanders.
Some of them were jealous of him, and he knew that they had plotted
toward his downfall. They did so because he did his job too well. His
company brought in the highest body counts, got the choicest informa-
tion out of captives. They kept the gooks in line, when other companies
were being overrun, kicked around like so much rabble. When the gen-
erals needed someone to salvage a snafu, they called on Rosky. In the
end, when a gang of deskbound pencil-pushers pulled the plug on him
to satisfy the liberal press, there was nothing left to do but kiss off eleven
years of faithful service and put his skills on the open market.

In *The Bone Yard* (Gold Eagle, 1985), one of the protagonists is an elderly
Jewish mobster whose Las Vegas territory has been gobbled up by Mafia
youngbloods. By the time we meet him, he's fed up and anxious for revenge
against his enemies:

Abe Bernstein was about to realize a dream he had been cherish-
ing for thirty years and more. Revenge required precision planning and
the father of Las Vegas had devoted three decades to winning back the
empire that was rightly his. Spinoza and his kind had ruled the roost
for too damn long already. It was time for them to settle up their debts.
In blood.

Another method of revealing motivation is by letting readers watch a character, observing his or her reactions and responses to a given situation.
Examine Thomas Bishop, in *By Reason of Insanity*, as he prepares for his
escape from the asylum:

Late at night in the privacy of his bed, alone in the bathroom or
on the grounds, whenever he had a moment to himself, he smiled and
laughed and raised his eyebrows and puckered his lips and widened his
eyes and made all the gestures of friendliness and innocence and sincer-

ity as he observed them in the attendants and on his obsession, TV. Whatever brought reward he adopted, whatever brought disapproval he discarded. In time he was thought to be improving, at least in his adaptability and social performance.

For all that he gained, however, there was an equivalent loss. He had no spontaneity, no feeling for the moment. His emotions were not tied to his body. He could smile while raging inside, he could laugh while in great pain. Sudden shifts in attitude or meaning always perplexed him and he had to be constantly on guard, ever watchful of others. He was a human robot who reacted to the emotions of others but could never act on his own feelings. In truth, he had no feelings and felt nothing. Except hatred. His hatred was monumental and encompassed virtually everything and everybody. But most of all, he hated where he was.

Description via Dialogue

Eavesdropping goes hand-in-hand with covert observation, and another way of picking a character's brain is through dialogue. Consider the delegation of Mafia authority as portrayed by Don Pendleton in *Chicago Wipeout*:

> "Why do you think I'm telling you all this, Turk?" the Capo asked. "And with these other two boys sitting right here listening in. Why do you think?"
>
> Turk didn't have to think. He knew. The thing was almost ceremonial—something pretty great was being conferred here tonight. He hesitated slightly, then replied, "I guess you're showing us your love for this thing of ours, Gio."
>
> "That's right, that's part of it. I don't love it this much, though, just because I'm the boss. It's the other way around. I'm the boss because I love our thing this much. Do you understand what I'm telling you?"
>
> "Yessir, and I appreciate the lesson, I really do."
>
> "Okay, don't mention it. But think about it. You think about it, and when you're done thinking you tell me what all this means to you."
>
> "I guess I can tell you right now, Gio."

"So?"

"So it's a damn shame you have to be a part of this dirt that's going on, and I don't like you being a part of it. By your leave, Don Gio, I'm taking full charge of things out here tonight. I don't want your mind bothered with such trash. With these two boys sitting here as witnesses, I'm saying that I take full responsibility for what goes on here at this place—and all over town, for that matter. However it comes out, I'm the one made the decisions."

In *Child of Blood*, I bring out a protagonist's naiveté in his conversation with a future victim:

"How long have you been out?"

Tony thought about the question, saw no need to lie. "Since six o'clock."

Vince giggled, leaning closer, placing one hand on his captured thigh. His touch made Tony's flesh crawl, reminding him of Esquivel.

"No, silly. I mean how long have you been out of the closet?"

Tony hoped that his bewilderment was not too readily apparent. "I was never in the closet."

Vince seemed impressed. "My God, I wish I'd had the courage of the youngsters coming out today. I mean, you can't imagine what it's like to hide your light beneath a bushel all through school. I didn't come out of the closet until I was twenty-three."

Convinced that he was in the presence of a madman, Tony thought it best to smile and hold his tongue.

It isn't necessary for a character to join in dialogue, however, for the spoken words of others to illuminate his character. Let's listen in as Dr. Frederick Chilton briefs Will Graham on the progress of an old nemesis, Hannibal ("The Cannibal") Lecter, in *Red Dragon*:

"It may seem gratuitous to warn you, of all people, about Lecter. But he's very disarming. For a year after he was brought here, he behaved perfectly and gave the appearance of cooperating with attempts at therapy. As a result—this was under the previous administrator—security around him was slightly relaxed.

"On the afternoon of July 8, 1976, he complained of chest pain. His restraints were removed in the examining room to make it easier to give him an electrocardiogram. One of his attendants left the room to smoke, and the other turned away for a second. The nurse was very quick and strong. She managed to save one of her eyes.

"You may find this curious," Chilton took a strip of EKG tape from a drawer and unrolled it on his desk. He traced the spiky line with his forefinger. "Here, he's resting on the examining table. Pulse seventy-two. Here, he grabs the nurse's head and pulls her down to him. Here, he is subdued by the attendant. He didn't resist, by the way, though the attendant dislocated his shoulder. Do you notice the strange thing? His pulse never got over eighty-five. Even when he tore out her tongue."

Interiors

If your characters aren't speaking, chances are they're thinking, and those thoughts can be extremely helpful in illuminating motives. Use of mental monologues, the "stream-of-consciousness" approach, can take your readers right inside the brains of heroes, heavies — anyone you choose to open up.

In *Cover* (Warner, 1987), author Jack Ketcham takes a look inside a veteran of Vietnam whose mind is slipping out of touch with those he loves, deserting hard-and-fast reality:

> *He looked at her, the wide blue eyes cast down, the mouth tight, the small thick hands busy breaking branches, snapping twigs.*
> *She's getting old, he thought. The brow furrows easily now.*
> *I'm making her old.*
> *He felt a familiar sudden access of rage and tenderness, fury and tears. He turned away.*
> *I cry so easily these days.*

Interiors can tell us more about a character than he or she is willing to confess aloud. Consider the haunting conclusion to Stephen King's "Strawberry Spring":

> *This morning's paper says a girl was killed on the New Sharon*

campus near the Civil War cannons. She was killed last night and found in a melting snowbank. She was not . . . she was not all there.

My wife is upset. She wants to know where I was last night. I can't tell her because I don't remember. I remember starting home from work, and I remember putting my headlights on to search my way through the lovely creeping fog, but that's all I remember.

I've been thinking about that foggy night when I had a headache and walked for air and passed all the lovely shadows without shape or substance. And I've been thinking about the trunk of my car—such an ugly word, trunk—and wondering why in the world I should be afraid to open it.

I can hear my wife as I write this, in the next room, crying. She thinks I was with another woman last night.

And oh dear God, I think so too.

A variation on the stream-of-consciousness technique involves quotation from the diaries or correspondence of specific characters. Occasionally, as in *Dracula* or Stephen King's "Survivor Type," a story may consist of nothing else. More often, journal entries and the like are placed strategically to offer shifting points of view and new perspectives on a character— her motivation, his behavior. Good examples can be found in works like *Carrie*, *Silent Terror*, and early novels in the *Executioner* series.

Whatever motivations you decide on, your characters must be credible in thought, action, and ability. Unless you're writing fantasy, your people must conform to all the laws of nature—and of *human* nature—in response to daily life or extraordinary challenges. A character need not be rational, per se, but neither should he change from nerd to Rambo in the twinkling of an eye. Your basic 98-pound weakling won't climb mountains, beat up on karate experts, or become a hero under fire, unless you've laid the necessary groundwork for the turn-around. A killer who despises women will need reasons for becoming suddenly infatuated with your heroine. Think twice before you have your people take a sex break in the middle of a life-and-death pursuit. Forget about those cartoon leaps from upper-story windows that have awnings down below.

I grant you, all these shoddy tricks have found their way to publication through the years, and some will doubtless be repeated in the future, by the lazy hacks who can't be bothered with a decent story line. Your readers won't appreciate cheap shots, believe me, and unless you've found yourself a publisher who gloats on trash — and pays accordingly — your editors won't like it, either. I assume that if you've come this far, you have an interest in producing works of *quality*. 'Nuff said.

Clichés and Propaganda

A common pitfall for beginners — and for many veteran authors — is reliance on a cast of characters who are, in fact, clichés. You know the type, from shiftless blacks to red-necked southern sheriffs, virginal librarians and whores with hearts of gold. We're talking *stereotypes* here, and if you're wise, you will avoid them like the plague.

Okay. Some real-life people *are* clichés, but in the realm of fiction they've been done to death. As a beginning writer — or beginning *genre* writer — you are out to make your mark with something new and different. You're also writing fiction, so you have a license to avoid the tired monotony of daily life and spice things up with some variety. Feel free to improvise. Surprise your audience, whenever possible, by putting new, unusual twists on old familiar characters. (Readers of *It*, by Stephen King, are 600 pages into the story before they learn a major character is black!)

Let's talk about the ladies for a minute, shall we? In the modern action novel, woman's place need not be strictly in the home — or in the bunker. Granted, females in the genre have been largely relegated to the roles of damsel in distress or luscious sidekick/bedmate to a macho man — Mack Bolan's April Rose, "Miss Paradise" in *Dennison's War*, Krysty Wroth in *Deathlands* — but the times are changing, guys. As noted earlier, some racy heroines have surfaced lately in the subgenre of adult Westerns, with respectable showings in single titles like *Flood*, *The Little Drummer Girl*, *The Third Deadly Sin*, *The Tuesday Blade*, *The Traveler*, and *The Passion of Molly T*. A survey of the literature would seem to indicate that members of the "gentle sex" can hold their own quite nicely, thank you, both as heroines *and* heavies.

While we're on the dark side, it is perfectly legitimate for you to deal with bigots, sadists, child abusers — name your poison — but you must beware of painting rabid deviants as heroes. I have seen it done successfully on one occasion, in a quirky murder yarn called *Killer on the Heights*, and even then the narrator, a racist vigilante, had to square accounts through an improbable (and poorly handled) suicide. If you insist on canonizing kooks and crazies, you not only jeopardize potential sales, but also risk offending major portions of your audience.

This doesn't mean your heavies can't have sympathetic traits — perhaps a member of the Klan who draws a private line at vandalizing churches, or a psychopath who suffered terrible abuse in childhood. Everybody has a past, and most (I won't say *all*) have good points, if you care to use a microscope, but don't lose sight of who and what these people are, in their relation to your tale.

(A brief time-out. I frankly have no interest in your politics, religion, nationality, or sex life. Writers are inevitably subject to the influence of factors in their private lives, but real professionals don't let it show in print. If you are simply looking for a propaganda forum, I suggest you don't belong in genre fiction. Check out *Writer's Market* for a sampling of the countless periodicals that trade in off-the-wall ideas, and find yourself a niche where you feel more at home.)

The Name Game

Once you have solid characters in mind — or, better yet, on paper — you must give them names. No problem? Guess again. Your choice of monikers for heroes, heroines, and heavies often sets the tone for everything that follows, shaping audience perception of the characters before your people have a chance to hit their stride.

What's in a name? Plenty! I hate to argue with the Bard, but I suspect a rose relies as much upon its label as its fragrance in the bid for popularity. Suppose, for instance, it was called a cactus (or a hemorrhoid!). The fact is, folks, there's something in the *sound*.

Author Thomas Millstead, in an essay on the christening of genre characters (*How to Write Tales of Horror, Fantasy & Science Fiction*, Writer's Digest Books, 1987), has prescient words of warning for the novice writer:

> The most quickly spotted tipoff to the amateur is the choice of names. . . . Too often they seem pinned on hastily, randomly, without purpose. They may be drab while the character is colorful. Or they may suggest ethnic or social backgrounds that have nothing to do with the characters or the narrative. Or several characters may have names closely resembling each other, sowing confusion.
>
> Above all, they don't ring true to the spirit or mood of the story.

They do not strum those subconscious chords that prompt the reader to suspend, unwittingly, all disbelief.

Admittedly, in real life our names may not ring true either. But in fiction too much disparity between name and persona can be lethally disruptive. The dominating precept is verisimilitude, a faithful wedding of narrative and name.

Or, simply stated, if the names don't fit, your characters may not fit, either.

Ian Fleming had a special knack for naming characters, his tongue-in-cheek approach producing classics that inevitably linger in the reader's mind when fine points of his plots are long forgotten. Hugo Drax. Jack Spang. Emilio Largo. Auric (i.e., "golden") Goldfinger. Ernst Stavro Blofeld. And the Fleming ladies! Dominoe Vitale. Tiffany Case. Vesper Lynd. Honeychile Rider. The incomparable Pussy Galore.

Names needn't be concocted with a leer in mind, however. In *The Dead Zone*, Stephen King deliberately calls his hero Johnny Smith to demonstrate that psychic trauma may be visited upon the most innocuous and ordinary of the species. Names like Bolan, Carter, Cody, Hawker, Lyons, Steele, and Stone may lack the Fleming poetry, but they possess a certain "ring" that suits the genre.

Back in Chapter 4, I noted that I often tag my characters with simple letters, in the place of names, while I'm constructing profiles. This does *not* mean you should name your people alphabetically, with Mr. Arnold chasing Mr. Bates, who loves Miss Coolidge, daughter of the late, lamented widow Dunn, and so forth. This is amateurish to the max, and editors will spot it in an instant. Likewise, as we learned from Millstead, you should not have Tommy Barnes and Tillie Bates pursuing Tony Baker through Bavaria. It gets too damned confusing, and if *you* can't tell your characters apart without a program, why should any of your readers care to try?

If perfect names suggest themselves the first time out, be thankful. If they don't, you needn't panic. Telephone directories will yield a crop of nifty surnames, everything from Aames to Zwissler. Major dictionaries frequently contain appendices of given ("Christian") names, complete with roots and ancient definitions. Failing that, there are innumerable "baby books," replete with names enough to staff an army.

Researching Heroes and Heavies

The creation of dramatic characters is your responsibility, but realism in the action genre may require at least a modicum of research. Bear in mind that many of your readers have extensive backgrounds in the military, law enforcement, or intelligence; they recognize mistakes in terminology, procedural behavior, weapons nomenclature, even uniforms – and many air their gripes in letters to the publisher. The chances are you won't be fired because you put the wrong patch on a uniform or place your hero in a nonexistent unit of the military, but habitual mistakes can be embarrassing, and they are easily avoided with a minimum of homework.

Thankfully, a wealth of published information is available on military life, covert intelligence collection and police procedures, paramilitary groups and counterterrorist activities . . . you name it. G-men, T-men, spooks and saboteurs, detectives, psychos, terrorists and gangsters; if it walks and talks, somebody, somewhere, has produced a book or article with all the background information you will need to make your characters compelling, lifelike. (While you're at it, keep in mind that one-time "heroes" – agents of the FBI or CIA, especially – are often cast as heavies since the seamy revelations of the latter 1970s. Feel free to break the mold and drop a ringer in from time to time.)

For military background on your heroes, check out Ian Padden's *Fighting Elite* series, published by Bantam Books. Individual volumes cover training, armament, and military actions undertaken by Marines, the Army Rangers, Air Commandos, and the rugged Navy SEALS. For decent coverage of forty-odd nations – including NATO signatories, Warsaw Pact, and nonaligned – consult *Uniforms of the Elite Forces*, by Leroy Thompson and Michael Chappell. Illustrations and text provide fairly detailed coverage of elite military units, from dress uniforms to specialized combat gear, weapons, and training. Also available, from Sterling Publications, is an eighteen-volume *Uniforms Illustrated* series, covering various nations and military eras through text and photographs.

Dealing with a foreign army? Not to worry. Some of the countless sources on the bookshelf include *March or Die*, by Tony Geraghty (French Foreign Legion); *Modern Elite Forces*, by David Miller; *Inside the Soviet Army Today*, by Steven Zaloga; *Warsaw Pact Ground Forces*, by Gordon Rottman; *Russia's War in Afghanistan*, by David Isby; and *GSG-9* (covering German counterterrorist activities), by Rolf Trophoven.

Few police agencies have been scrutinized as closely (or as critically) in recent years as the Federal Bureau of Investigation. The best study to date is Sanford Ungar's *FBI*, a comprehensive volume published in the wake of

Nixon's resignation, with particular attention given to the Bureau's areas of jurisdiction, investigative techniques, and chain of command. A fascinating inside view is found in William Sullivan's *The Bureau*, focusing on power politics within the FBI, while Nelson Blackstock covers dirty tricks in *COINTELPRO*. A dated, left-wing view of Bureau history is offered in *The FBI Nobody Knows*, by Fred J. Cook.

The CIA has sticky fingers in a thousand different pies, and agents of "the Company" are staples of adventure fiction, playing both sides of the street. Regardless of your viewpoint, you can get background information from many sources. David Wise and Thomas Ross created a sensation with *The Invisible Government*, a volume that has much to say about the first two decades of the CIA's covert activities. More valuable background is contained in *OSS: The Secret History of America's First Central Intelligence Agency*, by R. Harris Smith. Victor Marchetti and John Marks met strenuous opposition to publication of their volume, *The CIA and the Cult of Intelligence*, which remains informative despite numerous strategic deletions of "sensitive" material. The dark side of Agency business is plumbed by Charles Ashman in *The CIA-Mafia Link*, and by W. H. Bowart in *Operation Mind Control*. Bob Woodward brings matters immediately up to date in *Veil: The CIA's Secret Wars, 1981-1987*.

Foreign intelligence agencies have likewise received a wealth of exposure in recent years. David Wise and Thomas Ross followed their success in *The Invisible Government* with *The Espionage Establishment*, updating coverage on the CIA while tacking on surveys of intelligence gathering in Britain, China, and the USSR. The husband-wife team of Thomas Plate and Andrea Darvi provide a valuable resource volume in their *Secret Police*, and *The Hit Team*, by David Tinnin and Dag Christenson, offers an inside view of Israeli intelligence and counterterrorist activity. Michael Footner's *Interpol* examines the inner workings of a major international police network. A fascinating, if chaotic, overview of the intelligence community is offered by James Hougan in *Spooks*. For a peek behind the Iron Curtain, browse through John Barron's *KGB* and its sequel, *KGB Today*.

Mercenary soldiers figure prominently in the modern action genre, and the bookstores periodically abound with memoirs of various soldiers for hire. The single constant source of information on mercenary activities is, of course, *Soldier of Fortune* magazine, each issue packed with articles on tactics, weapons, and contemporary actions in a dozen "dirty little wars."

For an overview of the territory, check out *The Specialist*, by Gayle Rivers. Details of mercenary dress and armament are provided in Leroy Thompson's *Uniforms of the Soldiers of Fortune*. More specific sources include: *Mercenary*, by Mike Hoare; *The New Mercenaries*, by Anthony Mockler; and Peter MacDonald's *Soldiers of Fortune*.

Police procedures and organization are examined in a multitude of recent texts. The best all around is Jonathan Rubenstein's *City Police*. More detailed information on investigative tactics may be gleaned from the following volumes: *Fundamentals of Criminal Investigation*, by Charles O'Hara; Frank Patterson's *Manual of Police Report Writing*; *Homicide Investigations*, by Le Moyne Snyder; *Modern Criminal Investigations*, by Harry Soderman and John O'Connell; and *Techniques of Crime Investigation*, by Aren Svenson and Otto Wender.

The Gang's All Here

Villains, given their intrinsic liberation from the rules and regulations of polite society, are more diverse than their opponents on the side of law and order. Before progressing to specific criminal fraternities, you might peruse some general sources and acquire a feel for deviants in general, how they think and talk and act as they go merrily about their shady business. *Bloodletters and Badmen*, by Jay Robert Nash, is a pioneering encyclopedia of American crime, but watch out for numerous factual errors in the text. A better selection might be *The Encyclopedia of American Crime*, by Carl Sifakis. British author Colin Wilson has produced several reference works on the subject, including *Encyclopedia of Murder*, coauthored with Patricia Putnam, and a new *Encyclopedia of Modern Murder*, prepared with Donald Seaman. Casting modesty aside, I'll also recommend my own *Most Wanted*, an encyclopedic survey of the FBI's "Ten Most Wanted" fugitives, coauthored with my wife, Judy.

Traditional organized crime—i.e., "The Mafia"—provides a fair proportion of the heavies in contemporary action/adventure novels. Before you start blundering around in unfamiliar territory, tacking Italian names on all your villains and stuffing them with pasta, check out *The Mob*, by Virgil Peterson, for a survey of the multi-ethnic underworld. (Remember, we're avoiding those clichés!) Richard Hammer does a fair job of summarizing syndicate history in *Playboy's Illustrated History of Organized Crime*. The links between mobsters, corrupt unions, and modern political assassinations are examined in *The Hoffa Wars*, by Dan Moldea, and in David Scheim's *Contract on America*. Norman Lewis surveys the traditional Sicilian Mafia in *The Honored Society*.

In recent years, the old-line godfathers have faced stiff competition from new arrivals on the syndicate scene. Outlaw biker gangs are X-rayed, with telling effect, by Canadian author Yves Lavigne in *Hell's Angels: Taking Care of Business*. Chinese Triad societies get the treatment from Fenton Bresler in *The Chinese Mafia*, and from Sean O'Callaghan in *The Triads*. Japan's expanding syndicate is studied in *The Yakuza*, by David Kaplan and Alec Dubro, and in *The Tattooed Men*, by Florence Rome. International drug syndicates are examined in *The Underground Empire*, by James Mills, and in Alfred McCoy's *The Politics of Heroin in Southeast Asia*.

Terrorists are all the rage in modern action novels, and you ought to be acquainted with their tactics and philosophies. The best general sources are *The Terrorists*, by Christopher Dobson and Ronald Payne, *Brothers in Blood*, by Ovid Demaris, and *The Terror Network*, by Claire Sterling. Specific terrorist movements are targeted by Christopher Dobson in *Black September* (Palestinians), by Richard Gott in *Guerilla Movements in Latin America*, by Jillian Becker in *Hitler's Children* (the Baader-Meinhof gang), and by Tim Pat Coogan in *The I.R.A.* Stateside, the terrorist activities of Satanic cultists are reviewed by Maury Terry in *The Ultimate Evil*, and James Coates surveys modern neo-Nazis in *Armed and Dangerous*.

In the last analysis, however you decide to pair your heroes off against your heavies, they should be as big and bad and *real* as you can make them. If your characters don't "live," I guarantee your story won't.

Still with me? Great. So far, you've picked a story line, prepared an outline, and created living, breathing characters. It's not enough to simply have your people race around the countryside and shoot each other, though. They must communicate. And you, proud parent that you are, must teach them how to talk.

8. Say What?

Regardless of your story line, its setting, or the choice of characters, your novel *must* have dialogue. Case closed. It doesn't matter if your hero and his girlfriend have been mute from birth, they must communicate between themselves and with others, and the people who surround them must continue speaking in a normal fashion. There has never been, as far as I know, a successful "silent" novel, stripped of dialogue. If anything, such classics as *The Miracle Worker* and *The Heart is a Lonely Hunter*, dealing with mute protagonists, place even greater demands on their "normal" characters to carry the weight of the tale.

Some novice writers are intimidated by the thought of fabricating realistic conversations—*I* was—but the plain fact is, there's just no way around it. So, you've read some classy novels and decided for yourself that you can't measure up to dialogue prepared by Mailer, King, or Michener. Join the club. *They* didn't start out breaking records at the bookstore check-out counters, either—and they still draw barbs from critics when they fumble. (Don't believe me? Study the reviews of *It, Centennial*, or *Tough Guys Don't Dance*.)

Everybody starts as a beginner in the writing game, and every working writer polishes his work, his style, through practice. Read voraciously and type your fingers to the bone. Odds are, you'll get the hang of writing decent dialogue before you know it.

A Word on Basics

Because of manuscripts I've seen in slush piles (and in trash cans), I've decided to pause here for a brief review of English 101. Successful dialogue has style, but there are raw mechanics to be dealt with, too, and tons of style may not be adequate to cover faulty execution. Who will bother seeking hidden treasures in your work if your approach is semiliterate?

According to my dusty textbooks, there are three ways of constructing sentences with dialogue.

John said, "Throw down your gun and raise your hands."

"Throw down your gun," John said, "and raise your hands."

"Throw down your gun and raise your hands," John said.

Of course, I know you learned all this in junior high school, but it couldn't hurt to spend a moment studying the three examples, all the same. Note the positioning of punctuation marks, which periods and commas fall inside quotation marks, which fall outside. Your editor expects a few stray typos in a manuscript, but if you *always* get it wrong, he may suggest—and none too kindly—that you take your act to night school for a quick refresher on the basics.

As a rule, each speaker rates a separate paragraph, so your dialogue should come out looking something like:

"Throw down your gun," John said, "and raise your hands."
Bob dropped his pistol in the dust. "Where are you taking me?"
"We're going to the county jail," John snapped.

Some authors (and some editors) ignore this standard practice, but the end result can be a jumbled mess that leaves readers hopelessly confused regarding who said what to whom. In spite of the opinions aired by certain high-brow critics, awkward, murky prose is *not* a mark of classy writing. Rather, it is generally a sign of laziness and negligence.

A final word on dialogue mechanics, and we'll break for recess. Some quotation marks are single (') instead of double ("). These are used in dialogue to indicate a quote *within* a quote, as follows.

Tommy said, "I heard John shouting, 'Wait! Don't shoot!' "

Again, pay close attention to the placement of assorted punctuation marks, and don't reverse quotation marks by accident. They *are* reversed (with singular quotation marks beginning normal dialogue) in several foreign countries—chiefly Britain—and by certain publishers in the United States who seem to pride themselves on careless errors. Editors are, by and large, familiar with the rules of proper English. If you find yourself with an eccentric on your hands, intent on shifting all your punctuation marks around, my best advice would be to play it cool. (You've signed the contract, after all, and they *do* have the right to edit your material.) Do *not*, at any cost, give up your proper writing style. Next time around, the chances are a different editor will be delighted to receive a manuscript that's clean and literate in presentation.

Variety: The Spice of Life

You have probably encountered various "experimental" novels that dispense with normal punctuation, sentence structure, and the like. Their "freedom" may appeal to you, but think again before you try to crack the market with avant-garde manuscripts. Your safest bet, hands down, is to accept the standard rules of punctuation, learn them, and impress your editors with what a slick professional you are. There will be time enough to dabble in experimental prose when you've got several titles on the *New York Times* best-seller list and publishers are lining up around the block to bid against each other for your latest hot idea.

Concerned about the possibility of tedium in conversation circumscribed by rules? Relax. If you begin to feel confined by "Robert said" and "Jane replied," take heart. My handy desk thesaurus lists four double-column pages of alternatives to "said" and "say," from "argue" and "assert" to "wheedle," "wail," and "whine." (A note of caution, here. It's tempting, sometimes, to insert a different verb for every line of dialogue, but *don't*! Unless you've got a real dramatic point to make, simplicity is normally the safest way to go.)

The fact is, you're not obligated to identify your characters each time they speak. Max Franklin, in *The Dark* (Signet, 1978), presents two homicide detectives in discussion of an ex-con whose daughter has just been murdered:

> As the outer door closed behind Warner, Bresler asked, "Who'd he kill?"

"Guy in the sack with his wife."

"Her, too?"

Mooney shook his head. "Just him. How'd he take it?"

"Looking at the kid? Good enough, considering it was his only kid. Considering I didn't want to look at her again."

Mooney grunted.

"Not a bad dude," Bresler ventured.

Mooney glared at him. "Screw him," he said coldly.

In *Child of Blood*, my leading character, an Amerasian youth, encounters a belligerent policeman in a ritzy San Francisco neighborhood:

"You live around here, sport?"

As he plainly knew the answer before he asked the question, there seemed no point in lying.

"No, sir."

"Work around here, maybe?"

"No, sir." Thinking fast, he added, "I was visiting my uncle. He works there."

The officer ignored his offhand gesture toward the northern end of Parkwood Drive. "I'll needta see your driver's license."

"I don't have one," Tony answered truthfully. "I rode the train."

"The train?"

"BART."

"Mmm. Some other kinda I.D., then, let's go."

"My wallet is at home." He had no wallet, but it did not seem to matter now.

"Where's home?"

"I live on Mason Street."

"In Chinatown? You lost, or what?"

"I came to see my uncle," he repeated. "He works there."

"Yeah, yeah. I heard that. Has your uncle got a name?"

"Yes, sir."

"I'm waiting, boy."

"His name is Anh Nguyen."

"Vietnamese?"

"Yes, sir."

> "Must be a Yankee in the woodpile, huh? And you are?"
>
> "His nephew."
>
> "Your name."
>
> "Tony Giap."
>
> "Tony Jap?" The cop grinned maliciously. "I thought you were Vietnamese."

The lack of tag lines—"he said"; "she replied"—is perfectly acceptable, provided that your characters are readily identifiable without the tags.

Good dialogue is like the perfect introduction of a character: you know it when you read it, but it's not the kind of thing you can define, per se. We recognize good dialogue on sight—and sometimes recognize the other kind by smell—and yet there are no paint-by-number guidelines to ensure you get it right. It's trial and error, for the most part, but we *can* identify some elements of decent dialogue to help you in your quest.

Smooth Talk

For openers, dramatic dialogue should be both realistic and appropriate for characters in any given situation. Think about precisely who and what your people are, in relation to the story. How are they likely to address each other at their first meeting? Over dinner? While making love? As they prepare their weapons for a life-and-death engagement with the enemy?

As always, we can learn from bad examples. In an excerpt from *Behind the Door* (Warner, 1988), Frank Lambrith treats us to his version of an Ozark sheriff's deputy interrogating an employee of the local funny farm:

> "Mr. Rogers, the doctor has told you why we wanted to see you. It seems you're the last known person to see our ambulance."
>
> "Well, what does that make me, copper?"
>
> Mainwaring's voice developed a distinct chill. "Mr. Rogers, I would suggest that you adopt a more reasonable tone. I told you Skystone intends to cooperate with the local authorities in every way we can."
>
> In the lounge, the orderly assumed a smile that was more sickly than acceptable. "I'm sorry, sir. Guess I'm tired—didn't get a lot of sleep last night, either. What can I tell you?"
>
> Cobb opened his notebook. "The ambulance left here at about twelve forty-five—right?"

Rogers smiled again. It was a better effort, if not totally convincing. "Why, I couldn't rightly say. I know it was long enough before one o'clock for me to get back inside by then."

Cobb nodded. "You went outside to assist them backing out of the porte cochere and then followed them down the drive to take care of the gate. Is that correct?"

"Yes, sir. It's what Dr. Mainwaring told me to do, and I did it."

Let's forgive the plodding, awkward execution of the sample for a moment. Does it strike you as peculiar that two Ozark hill-dwellers, selected at random, would drop terms like "porte cochere" in normal conversation? Is its use in dialogue *appropriate*, considering the circumstances? (Usage isn't Lambrith's only problem here; he also leaves the mandatory hyphen out of "porte-cochere," and dumps its standard definition in an effort to insert some culture into his dialogue. The sanitarium described by Lambrith has no courtyard that would make the presence of his "carriage gate" a possibility.)

An awkward, pompous tone can murder dialogue, as amply demonstrated in Joe Rosenberger's *Slaughter in El Salvador* (Pinnacle, 1982):

"We might be able to give you more assistance if we knew the nature of your mission," Major Masmerta said decisively, his tone expectant.

"My orders are explicit." The Death Merchant turned to Donald Fey at the end of the table. "Not even Fey knows the nature of the mission, and he's the CIA Chief of Station here in San Salvador. For that matter, the Americans who will go with me are in the dark; they won't even see twilight until we reach Leon — sunlight when we get to Managua."

Compare that bulky sermonette with something more compact:

"You want to brief me on your mission?" Ryker asked.
The tall man shook his head. "It's need-to-know. You don't."

In two short lines, we've weeded out the excess verbiage, cut redundant introductions to established characters, and shed a pound or two of literary

104

chaff. Admittedly, we've also lost the "poetry" of twilight, sunlight, and the rest, but I suggest it's a loss we can afford to live with.

Bungled dialogue is like a pothole in the street; it jars your audience off course, and if the highway gets *too* rough, you may be left to finish on your own. In *Stone: M.I.A. Hunter* (Jove, 1987), author Jack Buchanan stumbles on a bit of conversation between mercenaries who've just rescued several American prisoners from enemy hands. As we join them, the POW's have refused to continue the march, and their benefactors — like the readers — are justifiably confused:

> "*Figure it out?*" *Loughlin asked.*
>
> "*Yep. Jack Mason, one of the M.I.A.'s, is dying. Tonight or tomorrow.*"
>
> "*So we pull back a few miles and wait?*"
>
> *Stone nodded.*
>
> "*Goddamn!*" *Wiley spat.*
>
> "*Our timing was terrible,*" *Loughlin said. He stood and turned away, shaking his head. "Where the bloody hell are those boots we brought? We had six pair spread out in packs. I'm going to find them and try to fit the guys.*"
>
> *Stone waved him on and Hog finished sharpening the small throwing knife from his boot before he stood.*
>
> "*I want to meet this Jack Mason.*"

What's wrong with this picture? Plenty. Since Loughlin, Stone, and Wiley have just rescued the captive Americans, is it really necessary for our hero to introduce Jack Mason as "one of the M.I.A.'s"? Who else is hanging around the camp, for pete's sake? Why does Loughlin say their timing was terrible? And why does he insert a minilecture on the missing boots, when everybody knows they brought six pairs along? (A subtle hint: we call it *padding*.)

Repetitious use of names in dialogue is hokey and distracting. Think about your normal conversations with a friend. How often do you call them by their given names while speaking face-to-face? ("Hello, Tom. Are you well, Tom? See you later, Tom.") And do you *ever* call them by their full names, as when Jack Buchanan has a hero's girlfriend tell him, "I've been waiting weeks to see you, Mark Stone"? We hear a lot of this on daytime soaps; it comes off sounding silly there, and it's no better when you put the words on paper.

Saying What You Mean

But enough, already. Now that we've examined what you *shouldn't* do, let's all enjoy some dialogue that works. In "Children of the Corn," we meet a married couple with some problems, courtesy of Stephen King:

> *Burt turned the radio on too loud and didn't turn it down because they were on the verge of another argument and he didn't want it to happen. He was desperate for it not to happen.*
>
> *Vicky said something.*
>
> *"What?" he shouted.*
>
> *"Turn it down! Do you want to break my eardrums?"*
>
> *He bit down hard on what might have come through his mouth and turned it down.*
>
> *Vicky was fanning herself with her scarf even though the T-Bird was air-conditioned. "Where are we, anyway?"*
>
> *"Nebraska."*
>
> *She gave him a cold, neutral look. "Yes, Burt. I know we're in Nebraska, Burt. But where the hell are we?"*
>
> *"You've got the road atlas. Look it up. Or can't you read?"*
>
> *"Such wit. This is why we got off the turnpike. So we could look at three hundred miles of corn. And enjoy the wit and wisdom of Burt Robeson."*

In King's skillful hands, the repetition of names serves a dual purpose, introducing new characters and clinching a tone of anger for the conversation.

In *Small World* (Macmillan, 1981), Tabitha King eavesdrops on a bitchy mother-in-law, plotting against her son's bride:

> *"Dear, dear Lucy," she purred. "She's so sweet."*
>
> *She shot a quizzical glance at Roger.*
>
> *"Doesn't she just make you want to gag?"*
>
> *Roger, loosening his tie, and trying to ignore seismic hunger pangs, sensed he was on shaky ground.*

"She's . . . cute," he said, covering himself with a word with notoriously broad shadings.

"Fat ass," Dolly pronounced. "Peasant."

It was unclear to Roger whether she meant her daughter-in-law or himself. Either way, he decided it was safer not to dignify it.

"Isn't it typical, though. Men. My son, marrying a woman so completely opposite to his mother."

If your aim is realistic dialogue, you have to know your people inside-out—their backgrounds, social status, present situations, any special slang or jargon used in their professions. Talking to yourself may help; feel free to act out different roles and get the feel of dialogue before it goes on paper. If the words ring true, the chances are you're doing fine. If not, you've still got ample time to start from scratch and get it right.

With Tongue in Cheek

A touch of humor couldn't hurt, from time to time, and when judiciously applied, it brightens up the darker moments of a melodrama. Watch as one of Robert Daley's slick D.A.s fends off a lawyer seeking leniency for a suspected rapist, in *Hands of a Stranger*:

"He comes from one of the best families in Pakistan," said the lawyer. "Have you had occasion to look into his family connections as yet?"

"I knew there was something I meant to do," said Judith, and she watched him.

The fat man gave another laugh. "I happen to know he's very well connected. You may recall the name Prime Minister Zia?"

"My knowledge of Pakistan politics is a little weak," said Judith.

"My client's family and the prime minister's family are like that."

"As close as that?"

"Closer. The prime minister—he's like a second father to him."

"Have you checked into all this?" murmured Judith. "You didn't just get it from him?"

"Would you recall who happens to be the minister of defense back there in Pakistan?"

"I used to know," said Judith, "but I forget."

In John Katzenbach's novel, *The Traveler* (Ballantine, 1988), detective Mercedes Barren interviews a serial killer suspected of slaying her niece:

> *"I have nightmares," he said.*
> *"You damn well ought to," replied Detective Barren.*
> *"I see faces, people, but I cannot recall their names."*
> *"I know who they are."*
> *Tears started to form in the corners of his eyes and he rubbed at them.*
> *"God is not with me. No longer, no longer. I am abandoned."*
> *"Maybe he wasn't so damned pleased with what you were doing."*
> *"No! He told me!"*
> *"You misunderstood."*
> *Rhotzbadegh paused. He produced a tattered handkerchief from a pocket and blew his nose three times hard.*
> *"This," he said in a tone suffused with despair, "is a possibility."*

A major part of writing decent dialogue is learning what to jettison along the way to final copy. Realism doesn't mean your dialogue should mirror daily conversation, with its small talk, lengthy pauses, hemming, hawing, and redundancies. ("Uh, gee, Frank, I don't think . . . no, let me see . . . I mean . . . well, gosh. . . . ") That's *boring*, and a flagrant waste of time. If you don't learn to trim the dead wood early on, your editor will have to do it later. (That's assuming she still cares enough to take the time.)

Techno-Babble

The dialogue in modern action novels often tends to specialize in military jargon, weapons nomenclature, coded names for high-tech hardware, and the like. Law enforcement jargon poses special problems of its own, as in this excerpt from *Blood Testament* (Gold Eagle, 1987):

> *"Hal's in deep. He needs a specialist."*
> *"Explain."*
> *"His family's been taken, and the brass at Justice have him figured for a mole."*

108

"That's bullshit."

"Hey, I know that, but they're talking evidence. Like phone logs, videos, the whole nine yards."

You'll need to be conversant with the special language your characters would logically employ in any given situation. Much of what you need will be available from sources named in Chapter 6; the basic firearms nomenclature, details on equipment, vehicles and such, can be extracted from the references I list in Chapters 9 and 10. For basic, CIA-type jargon, I recommend Bob Burton's *Top Secret: A Clandestine Operator's Glossary of Terms*. The common slang of grunts in Vietnam is found in handy glossaries appended to *The Thirteenth Valley* or to episodes of the *Chopper 1* and *Vietnam: Ground Zero* series. Relevant law enforcement terms are contained in an appendix to Sanford Ungar's *FBI*. Depending on your subject matter, scientific, medical, and legal dictionaries may provide that extra touch of realism to your dialogue.

Translation, Please

Ironically, some problems arise when authors strive too hard for realism, flair, or drama in their dialogue. One common pitfall is the overuse (i.e., abuse) of foreign words and phrases in a bid to make the readers think they're really listening to Arabs, Orientals, Africans—whatever. The results can be effective or disastrous, depending on the way a writer handles his material. Remember that a storyteller's job is to communicate, and if you don't accomplish that, you've failed your audience. There may be nifty little jokes or subtle clues concealed beneath the foreign phrases you employ, but if your readers never get the point, who cares?

Most authors fall back on assorted dictionaries, phrase books, and the like for foreign phrases, and it shows more often than it should. Be cautious here. It doesn't hurt to have a Spanish character respond with "sí" instead of "yes" from time to time, but if you catch him rattling on for paragraphs, you ought to think again. If foreign phrases serve no purpose in your story—i.e., if they've been inserted as the springboard for an ego trip, to make the author (you) sound more sophisticated—they should be discarded. Likewise, if you have to salt the text with parenthetical translations, footnotes, and the like, you would be well advised to stick with English from the start.

The use of dialects and accents may be useful in establishing your characters—but it can also blow up in your face, unless you're careful. Cousin Timmy's fretting over pore ole Aunt Cecilia, livin' by her lonesome in the holler? Good for him. But bear in mind that unfamiliar dialects, when overused, have a potential for confusing readers. Worse, if the colloquial expressions overlap your mainstream narrative, outside established dialogue, the *author* may begin to seem illiterate. Don't have your people runnin', jumpin', and the like, in mainstream narrative unless the point of view has clearly been established for a character who *would* think in those terms. (Be cautious, all the same. Editors are prone to have even their illiterate characters *think* in proper English.)

Expletives Deleted?

Obscenity goes hand-in-hand with dialect and slang. There are no rules, per se, about insertion of profanity in dialogue, but tiresome repetition of "the F word" and its cousins can be self-defeating for a writer. Hard-core language is, ideally, used to make a point: to shock, surprise, or have some other predetermined impact on your readers. Well-timed expletives, evoked from characters who otherwise would never let such language pass their lips, can have a powerful effect in dialogue. But if we've grown accustomed to the use of "fucking" this and "frigging" that in every other line, what happens to the impact? Pfft! It's gone.

I dare say most of us know real-life individuals who can't complete a sentence, let alone a paragraph, without resort to certain pet obscenities. Are any of them *really* interesting? No? So, why should your prospective readers care to take them home, and pay you for the privilege, at that? Keep your swear words sparse and they'll gain impact.

But don't shy away from blunt language, either. Action heroes don't say "Drat"; vicious terrorists don't scream "Phooey!" Although sexist and racist slurs should be avoided, it's natural that the occasional four-letter word will slip out in the heat of battle. Either *use* the word or else cut profanity and obscenity altogether: accept no substitutes.

When fledgling authors strive for color and variety in dialogue, they sometimes run afoul of misused "onomatopoeia" (words that imitate the sounds they describe). Action scenes are frequently enlivened with the *clang* of steel on steel, the *buzz* of insects, or the *crack* of rifle fire. It works, but writers sometimes lose control as characters begin to grunt, groan, snap, and snarl in lieu of simply saying what is on their minds. The curse of misused onomatopoeia strikes when careless writers fasten on a catchy verb without regard to its appropriate employment in the text.

"Get out!" he hissed.

Perhaps, but I'm inclined to doubt it. Hissing deals with sibilance, the airy, lisping sound that we associate most commonly with serpents in the grass. "Get out!" has none of that, and "hissed," therefore, is badly out of place as a description of the utterance.

"She stole my wallet," Tommy moaned.

Not likely. Moaning is a sound of pain, and normally an inarticulate response to pain, at that. I question whether *any* sentence can be moaned, and clearly, the example cited does not fit the bill.

"I thought you might forget your flashlight," Amy chuckled, "so I brought an extra."

Can you really picture anybody *chuckling* a twelve-word sentence? They would certainly be incoherent, and might well be taken for a mental patient out on furlough. Either way, the author's choice of verbs is ill-advised. Before you wax poetic in your dialogue, be sure your phrase of preference makes sense in context. Otherwise, your readers may be chuckling when you expect them to be hissing—and the laugh will be on you.

We've already dealt with the desirability of avoiding stereotypical characters, but the message bears repeating here, in reference to dialogue. Dramatic conversations are a vital part of character depiction; you should exercise restraint in use of "ethnic" dialects and accents, which may jeopardize an otherwise dynamic character, transforming him or her into a tired cliché.

Clichés Revisited

A character who happens to be black and earns a million dollars yearly will not talk like Stepin Fetchit in a movie from the 1920s. "I'se gwan home now, suh," won't make it anymore. Hispanics may occasionally sound like Cheech and Chong in concert—"Man, tha's some charp car joo got dere"—but for every one who does, there are a dozen who do not. I seriously doubt that any Native Americans have referred to "white man speaking with forked tongue" in recent years, and woe to any author who depicts a leader of the Yakuza buying "rorrypops" for his children, sipping "chelly Coke," or rushing home from work to see his "Mama-san." If your ethnic sensitivity extends no further than your bank book, bear in mind that you cannot predict the nationality or background of prospective editors and publishers. If you offend them going in, you're out of work.

Sexual clichés are also tacky, though your average action editor is quicker to forgive depiction of a fluffy female airhead than he would be an attack on Blacks or Jews. Remember, please, that while your basic macho man is still a staple of the genre, your protagonist is not required to be a neolithic chauvinist. Examine, if you dare, the suave technique of J. C. Stonewall, *Soldier for Hire*, as he puts his move on "the only white woman in Singapore":

> *"You're a gorgeous broad, Audry. And I simply wanted to buy you a glass of champagne."*
> *"And?"*
> *He shrugged. "And take you out to a late supper and then to bed."*

The lady's response? What else? She heads for the nearest hotel room, drops her clothes and cries, "You are the stuff of my dreams, J. C. Hurry, fill me with that enormous phallus before I lose my cookies right here."

Heard enough? I thought so. Never mind the critical dissection of a scene like this. The best that it deserves is speedy burial. In an apparent effort to fulfill some adolescent fantasy, the author makes his characters— and then himself—look foolish in a classic case of lazy, heavy-handed writing. (And *what* writing! Last time I heard someone say they were about to "lose their cookies," they were suffering from nausea. In Audry's case, it must be shock induced by that "enormous phallus.")

On the distaff side, I realize that women, for the most part, still play second string in action novels, but they are increasingly portrayed as levelheaded, competent professionals. The ladies aren't just pretty airheads anymore, and women who display a competence with weapons or computers needn't be portrayed as lesbians or frigid spinsters, either. On the other hand, despite the harsh realities of life around the U.S. Embassy in Moscow, female agents are not universally required to put their bodies on the line for every mission they accept. The luscious agent sleeping with a mobster/commie/Nazi/terrorist for information has been done to death; it may have uses, now and then, but it deserves a rest.

The Author as a "Silent Partner"

It's tempting, sometimes, to employ your characters as spokesmen for your own philosophy. Most authors tip their hands from time to time through dialogue, a passing comment, their depiction of a character. It's natural, and it shouldn't be a problem if you exercise a little self-restraint. We hit a snag when propaganda takes the place of fiction, and the author's personality distorts his story line. As noted earlier, it's fine to let a racist character express himself through dialogue, as long as readers understand he doesn't speak for *you*. When the distinction is obliterated, you've got problems on your hands.

Let's take another look at J. C. Stonewall, brainchild of author Mark Roberts in the now-defunct *Soldier for Hire* series. The ultimate chauvinist, Stonewall is also a pathological red-baiter, incessantly cursing New York liberals (i.e., Jews), gun-control advocates, and "those fuckin' ragheads in Iran." At one point, after nearly drowning, Stonewall rails against the sea for its temerity in trying to stop him "from killing more commies." His personal bogeyman is "Senator Ned Flannery," a transparent stand-in for a well-known eastern politician, as depicted in the following excerpt from *Jakarta Coup* (Zebra, 1983):

> "At least he won't be running for president," Theo observed.
> "Don't fucking count on it," Stonewall snapped. "He said the same thing last time, then campaigned like mad for it. It was the same old shit four years before that. He's just angling to get the loyal party hacks to beg him to take the nomination."
> "The Flannerys do seem to think they are the rightful pretenders to the throne of North America," Ed allowed.
> "Yeah. King Ned the First," Stonewall shot back. "King of the sewer rats if you ask me."

A browse through any novel in the Stonewall series makes it obvious that

113

J. C., by and large, is speaking on behalf of his creator. It gets tiresome in a hurry, and an author who insists on lecturing his readers in the guise of fiction should prepare himself for ultimate (and well-deserved) rejection in the marketplace.

Politically, adventure fans are normally conservative. That *doesn't* mean, however, that your readers are a pack of hard-core, neo-Nazi morons. If your novels come off sounding like the latest issue of *The Fiery Cross*, you have a problem on your hands. As Stephen King has aptly stated, "It's the tale, not he who tells it."

Decent dialogue, in short, is crucial to development of characters and to advancement of a story. If perfection of technique requires some sweat in the beginning, you should find it worth your time and effort in the end. It's not enough, however, for your characters to simply walk and talk. In action novels, there is always dirty work afoot, and having come this far, it's time to brace yourself for fighting fire with fire.

9. "Gunpowder Orgies"

Wherever genre publishing is open to debate, the "sex-and-violence problem" rears its ugly head. Like gun control or the women's movement, it raises hackles, sparking angry diatribes from "intellectuals" who fail to recognize a phony issue when they see one. Still, the genre and its authors take a lot of flack for their alleged promotion of a sexist, trigger-happy atmosphere in the United States, and no discussion of the genre is complete without a look behind the florid rhetoric.

The general tone for critical response to action novels was established in the early 1970s by a review in *New Republic*. Dishing up a survey of the field, then ruled by Pinnacle, the author took a clumsy stab at social criticism, lumping various genre entries together as "gunpowder orgies." A decade later, SMU Professor William Gibson still bemoans the presence of a "paramilitary culture" in America, sustained by literature he describes as "cheap, formula written and erotic." Interviewed by the *Chicago Tribune* (August 27, 1987), Gibson set his sights on action heroes, offering the sage opinion that "Sex is not far from their violence."

Enough, already. If you've heard one critic blast the genre, you have literally heard them all. This book is not the place to argue psychiatric theories of the gun as phallic symbol, and I will not bore you with my personal opinions of the self-appointed censors who insist on blaming television, books, and movies for the actions of assorted violent misfits. Let's just say that murder, rape, and torture were "invented" long before the printing press, the movie camera, or the VCR, and I suspect these pastimes will endure when technology has turned another page. The fact is, sex and violence *do* exist in genre fiction, and if you pursue your interest in the field, you will inevitably have to deal with both.

115

More Mayhem, Please

For starters, we must realize that "action" and "adventure" are not necessarily synonymous. A reference to "action" currently implies a fair amount of violence, often lethal, frequently described in graphic terms. If you're uncomfortable with the idea of killing people on paper, you should seriously think about some other field of fiction where you won't be forced to deal with violence so directly.

Readers in the action genre come prepared to cope with sex and violence, but their personal responses vary widely. A New Jersey woman in her twenties writes Gold Eagle, publishers of *The Executioner*, that she's "pleased that sex is kept to a minimum in this action-adventure series." A man in his sixties complains that action novels "don't need such graphic descriptions of the effect of bullets and knives." On the flip side, a teenage boy laments that there's "not enough violence" in recent offerings, and a female reader in her late sixties echoes his complaint. "There was not enough VIOLENCE," she writes. "Add more descriptions of wounds!"

Which brings us to the classic question: How much violence is *too* much? Is violent content to be judged by graphic scenes, or on the basis of accumulated body-counts? And who decides?

There is a world of difference between the splatter novels, typified by Jack Ketcham's *Off Season*, and more restrained offerings like Tom Harris's *Red Dragon*, where most of the violence is implied (or at least spared graphic depiction). Both styles have their followings, and I believe both authors are sincere in their attempts to entertain a given audience. The ultimate selection of a style for handling violence will depend, in fairly equal measure, on the author's private taste and on his editor's discretion.

Unless your contract grants you editorial approval — and it won't, unless your prior sales have placed you in the tiny "household name" fraternity of million-selling authors — final content of your novels will be thrashed out by the editors, who rule on everything from general themes to the specific punctuation marks and choice of language in a given snatch of dialogue. Occasionally, editors may wish to punch up a sluggish story by adding further action scenes — and some still cherish quotas that demand a given quantity of violence per manuscript — but more are likely to concern themselves with the varieties and specificity of mayhem than its frequency.

Gold Eagle's editors maintain a policy of toning down (or cutting out) sadistic torture scenes, and they are not alone. Deletion of repulsive violence strikes the great and small alike, as shown by Stephen King in *Danse Macabre* (Everest House, 1981), when he discusses the strategic use of hungry rats:

> *Actually, I used them to create a scene so revolting that my editor suggested strongly that I remove it and substitute something else. After some grousing, I complied with his wishes. In the Doubleday/New American Library editions of 'Salem's Lot, Jimmy Cody, a local doctor, and Mark Petrie, the boy accompanying him, discover that the king vampire — to use Van Helsing's pungent term — is almost certainly denning in the basement of the local boarding house. Jimmy begins to go downstairs, but the stairs have been cut away and the floor beneath littered with knives pounded through boards. Jimmy Cody dies impaled upon these knives in a scene of what I would call "horror" — as opposed to "terror" or "revulsion," the scene is a middle-of-the-roader.*
>
> *In the first draft manuscript, however, I had Jimmy go down the stairs and discover — too late — that Barlow had called all the rats from the dump to the cellar of Eva Miller's boarding house. There was a regular HoJo for rats down there, and Jimmy Cody became the main course. They attacked Jimmy in the hundreds, and we are treated (if that is the word) to a picture of the good doctor struggling back up the stairs, covered with rats. They are down his shirt, crawling in his hair, biting his neck and arms. When he opens his mouth to yell Mark a warning, one of them runs into his mouth and lodges there, squirming.*
>
> *I was delighted with the scene as written because it gave me a chance to combine Dracula-lore and E.C.-lore into one. My editor felt that it was, to put it frankly, out to lunch, and I was eventually persuaded to see it his way. Perhaps he was even right.*

Ego aside, they usually are. If editors tone down your violence, they probably have some reason other than personal squeamishness — i.e., company policy, or an aversion to offending their readers with gratuitous gore and sadism. It may smart a bit when your pet scenes are trimmed to the bone, but remember the editor shares your responsibility for producing a polished, quality book.

Killing 'em Softly

Stylistic handling of violence varies with the personality of each and every writer in the business. Savvy authors realize it pays to give their readers some variety, adopting different angles of attack from time to time. Examine how Tom Harris leaves the killing carefully off stage in this example from *Black Sunday*:

> *Number 18 Rue Verdun was guarded round the clock. One sentry was stationed in the foyer, and another armed with a machine gun watched from the roof of the building across the street. Now the rooftop sentry lay in a curious attitude behind his gun, his throat smiling wetly in the moonlight. The sentry from the foyer lay outside the door where he had gone to investigate a drunken lullaby.*

But Harris can explode, when mayhem is required, as in *Red Dragon*, when we see the last of killer Francis Dolarhyde:

> *She forgot the stance and she forgot the front sight but she got a good two-handed grip on the pistol and as the door exploded inward she blew a rat hole through his thigh — "Muhner!" — and she shot him in the face as he slid down the door facing and she shot him in the face as he sat on the floor and she ran to him and shot him twice in the face as he sprawled against the wall, scalp down to his chin and his hair on fire.*

Don Pendleton is another author well versed in the variations of violent delivery. Examples of the "hard" and "soft" approach are found within a dozen pages of each other in his novel *Nightmare in New York*. We meet the Executioner as he discovers that a female ally has been tortured by the mob:

> *He stepped jerkily to the table and gazed down upon what was left of Evie Clifford. The dead eyes stared back at him. They had to. The eyelids had been sliced away. And even through the coagulated blood that was brimming those horrified sockets Bolan could see the agony and the accusation and the mirror of his own guilt and neglect.*

*They had battered out her front teeth and committed awful atroc-
ities upon the once lovely torso, and what they had done below that
point sent Bolan's usually steady mind on a spin through insanity.*

*His chin dropped to his chest, his eyes closed on the terrible scene,
and he groaned, "Oh . . . God!"*

*Then he went down to the screeching man and shoved the hot
muzzle of the chattergun into the wide open mouth and he pulled the
trigger and let the gun burp until the clip was empty, and somewhere
in there the screaming stopped. He dropped a marksman's medal into
the gaping well of blood, and reloaded, and went deliberately from body
to body and repeated the routine.*

A few pages later, Bolan launches a blitz against the New York "family,"
which is subdued by comparison, and seasoned with a cautious touch of
humor:

*Twenty minutes later he struck again, this time at the Manhattan
offices of Schweiberg, Fain, and Marksworth — purportedly an invest-
ment brokerage firm but actually the funnel through which Gambella's
illicit wealth was spread into the legitimate business world. The firm
went abruptly out of business at 11:22 A.M. that Wednesday in Decem-
ber, the partnership dissolved by mutual death, its records consumed
by a fire of incendiary origin. Again, a tall man in army fatigues and an
OD field jacket pressed a marksman's medal into the shaken palm of
a female employee before he calmly departed the scene.*

*At a few minutes past noon, in the back room of a neighborhood
restaurant on 144th Street, a weekly "business luncheon" of the Upper
Manhattan Protective League was disrupted by an obvious lack of pro-
tection. This group, consisting of neighborhood politicians and muscle-
men, was severely depleted of active membership by the sudden appearance of two fragmentation grenades on the menu. A tall man in
army combat dress settled the property damages with a thousand dollars in cash and a marksman's medal.*

Whenever possible, I try to find a happy medium between anatomy and
art. I won't pretend it always works, but practice makes its easier, as in
the following encounter from *Doomsday Disciples* (Gold Eagle, 1983):

Bolan took the nearest gunner first, his Beretta chugging out a
pencil line of flame. The 9mm parabellum sizzled in on target, punch-
ing through a tanned cheek under the right eye, expanding and reaming
on, exiting with a spray of murky crimson. The impact spun him like
a top and dumped him facedown on the carpet.

His partner had an autoloader out and tracking Bolan when Belle
coughed a second time. The gunner lurched backward as a parabellum
mangler pierced his throat, releasing a bloody torrent from his ruptured
jugular. For an instant he was frozen, gagging on his own vital juices;
his lips worked silently, emitting scarlet bubbles.

Bolan again stroked the trigger and again silent death closed the
gap between them, exploding in the gunner's face. A keyhole opened
in his forehead and the lock was turned, explosively releasing all the
contents of that dark Pandora's box. Bits and pieces of the guy were
outward bound before his body got the message, rebounding off the sofa
on its way to touchdown.

Mayhem Mechanics

Several pitfalls are commonly encountered in construction of a violent
scene, and would-be authors ought to recognize each one of them on sight.
Resort to formulaic, set-piece at established intervals throughout a story
may appear to give your manuscript a certain balance, when, in fact, it
merely makes the tale predictable and dull. It's fine to have your hero face
a hostile army every now and then, but if he does it every other chapter,
making his escape like clockwork, readers will experience a nagging sense
of déjà vu.

Another common blunder is the overuse of certain "catchy" words or
phrases to distinguish action scenes. Let's examine a classic fumble from
The Ninety-Nine (Gold Eagle, 1984):

Track dropped the shotgun to hip level and rammed the five
rounds from his Perry sling, one at a time, into the magazine tube. He
guessed blindly that the tube had six rounds left. He tromboned the
pump, shouldered it again and sighted over the front blade. He fired,
tromboned; fired, tromboned; fired, tromboned; fired.

He wheeled half left. Two of the nearest Bedouin horsemen broke
off to outflank him. Their assault rifles spit orange tongues of flame,

and the slugs kicked up sand at his feet. He tromboned *the pump, fired—one horseman down; then* tromboned *the action again, firing—the second rider down. Track pumped the action, and the red high-brass shell sailed out of the ejection port. Nothing in the chamber.* [Emphasis added.]

Now, don't get me wrong. I've got nothing against the trombone, but this is overkill. Afraid some readers may have missed his point, the author takes a clever turn of phrase and hammers it into the ground. By the end of the second paragraph, he's beating a dead horse.

Another frequent failing is the amateurish fallback into "cartoon" violence, characterized by impossible leaps and kicks, miraculous trick shots, or guns with inexhaustible supplies of ammunition. You don't need a Ph.D. in math to know a weapon holding twenty rounds won't stop a hundred men without reloading several times, and if your hero's stopped a bullet in the chest, he shouldn't plan on running any marathons.

The flip side of the cartoon syndrome is compulsive technicality, with authors reeling off the caliber and model number, muzzle velocity and magazine capacity for every gun in every scene. It's nice to add a touch of authenticity from time to time, but no one wants to sit and read a catalogue of MAC 11s, M-16s and AK-47s, RPGs, SPAS-12s, and Model 1911A1s. Before you lose your story—and your readers—in a cloud of nomenclature, take a break and call a spade a spade . . . or, call a *gun* a *gun*.

Shopping for Hardware

Speaking of firearms, you don't have to be a gun buff or a combat veteran to write successful action scenes, but if you're ignorant concerning weapons, you will have to cure your deficiency through homework. Do it *now*, before your readers start bombarding editors with post cards pointing out the errors in your work.

You think I'm kidding? Bear in mind that many members of your audience are military veterans or law enforcement officers. They know their hardware inside out, and they are not above complaining when an author gets the details wrong. It's easy for an editor to miss a small mistake in nomenclature, caliber—whatever—but your readers don't miss *anything*.

I grant you, firearms technicalities may not seem crucial to the story, but they add up, all the same. When Adam Lassiter, in *Triangle*, makes reference to the "two firing handles" on an M-60 machine gun, it sounds convincing. Unfortunately, there is no such mechanism on the weapon, as the author could have learned by simply glancing at a photograph. When Mark K. Roberts has a Russian AK-47 rifle firing 5.56mm rounds, midway through *Jakarta Coup*, it's no big deal—except to fans who know damn well the weapon chambers 7.62, instead. They mull the passage over for a while and grumble to themselves—and some of them sit down to write the publisher in protest. Again, I've never heard of any writer being canned for careless errors, but enough of them will definitely blow your reputation as a master of your craft.

I wish I had a dime for every time I've caught a character in "brand name" novels playing with the safety switch on his or her revolver. Why? *Because there's no such thing!* I'm sorry, folks, but it's a fundamental fact of life: revolvers don't have safeties; automatics *do*. And while we're on the subject of impossibilities, you cannot detonate a stick of dynamite by firing at it with a gun. What's that? You *saw* Clint Eastwood do it in the *movies*? Sorry, folks. Do not attempt this trick at home.

Another piece of hardware that has scuttled many authors is the so-called silencer. Professionals refer to these devices as suppressors, out of recognition for the fact that no effective firearms silencer has been invented. Certainly, they help to muffle gunshots, if attached correctly to the proper weapons, but you can forget about portrayals of the silencer in movies and on television. Sound-effects technicians have been working overtime to make those babies whisper. (When a gang of modern neo-Nazis murdered Alan Berg in 1984, they used a silencer. According to the transcripts of their trial, the weapon, made professionally, still produced a sound like someone slamming down a heavy dictionary on a desktop.)

R. Lance Hill presents a fine, authentic-sounding picture of a silenced weapon in *The Evil That Men Do* (Bantam, 1978):

> *Having begun life as a quite ordinary Smith and Wesson Model 57 revolver in .41 magnum caliber, the firearm had then undergone more than a hundred hours of work in order for it to suit Holland's exacting standards: fitted with a custom five-inch barrel, muzzle vented and sufficiently heavy to reduce recoil . . .*
>
> *Also in the case was a silencer. Silencers by their proper designation are called "suppressors," most being woeful devices severely hin-*

dering the effectiveness of the firearm they are coupled to, restricting the bullet's velocity as well as adversely affecting the accuracy because of vibrations. They are deplored for fouling the gun barrel with spent powder, many not suppressing the report of the gun so much as redirecting the noise indiscriminately. However, the suppressor Holland employed was the latest in applied technology and not only did all that a suppressor was designed to do, but in practice actually enhanced the velocity of the bullet passing through its titanium embrace.

Convincing, right? Unfortunately, Hill is blowing smoke across the board. For starters, it's impossible to "silence" a revolver, since the sound and flash of every shot escape through open space around the cylinder. Next problem: The description of a "vented" barrel simply means there have been holes cut near the muzzle, to reduce a weapon's kick. If vents are covered by a silencer, they do no good, and if they're *not*, the sound of every shot escapes as if there were no silencer in place. To round things off, Hill has a basic problem with his choice of ammunition. Many bullets travel faster than the speed of sound, like tiny fighter planes, and make another racket independent of their weapon once they leave the muzzle. No attachment can suppress this secondary noise, and so the active candidates for silencing are limited to guns that fire projectiles at subsonic speeds — that is, slower than 1,100 feet per second. Your average .41 magnum round leaves the muzzle at 1,500 feet per second, and Hill's technology makes it travel even *faster*, indicating that his supergun should be about as quiet as a cannon in a closet.

If you're a novice in the field of firearms, you can depend on countless sources to keep you on the straight and narrow once you've done your homework. *Guns and Ammo* is the best of several monthly magazines devoted to the shooting sports, including articles on new developments in weapons, ammunition, and the handling of same. The classic reference works are *Small Arms of the World*, now edited by Edward Ezell, and its companion volume, *Sporting Arms of the World*, by Ray Bearse. Both provide comprehensive coverage of weapons available to civilians and military personnel, complete with ballistics tables, instructions for field stripping and cleaning, the history of firearms development, and so forth. Other handy volumes include David Rossner-Owen's *Vietnam Weapons Book*, George Markham's *Guns of the Elite*, and Frank Moyer's *Special Forces Foreign Weapons Handbook*. Two volumes by Duncan Long, *Combat*

Ammunition and *Streetsweepers* (a treatment of combat shotguns), round off the basic firearms library in fine style.

Weapons nomenclature may be half the battle, but your characters will still look silly if they don't know how to handle all those M-14s, MAC 10s, and what-not. Personal experience is still the best foundation for authentic writing; if you've never fired a gun, you really ought to try it. Chances are your relatives or friends have hardware stashed away that you could borrow; if they don't, some firearms outlets (like the Survival Store, in Las Vegas) rent weapons and range time to interested parties, offering instruction and supervision in the handling of anything from pistols to submachine guns.

Barring close encounters with a "real, live" gun, you can absorb a measure of the necessary knowledge secondhand. Jeff Cooper's *Principles of Personal Defense* is a useful volume for beginners. Chuck Taylor has two useful books on the market: *Combat Handgunning* and *The Combat Shotgun and Submachine Gun*. For sniper tactics, consult *Sniper/Counter Sniper*, by Mark Lonsdale. The techniques of street survival are examined by Massad Ayoob in *Stressfire* and its companion volume, *In the Gravest Extreme*.

Down and Dirty

Action, unlike Rap Brown's definition of political power, does not always issue from the barrel of a gun. Your heroes may be forced to deal with villains hand-to-hand, and when they do, you must take pains to keep the combat scenes authentic. If you're writing martial arts, you might consider signing up for classes — or at least observing some. Do *not* rely on wacky kung fu films or published fiction for your background information; both are riddled with inaccuracies and impossible performances by characters who leap around like Superman, defying gravity and every other law of nature as they take on armies single-handed. Every major bookstore carries manuals on martial arts, most often tucked away with the biographies of football stars and volumes on aerobics. If you're looking for a little something "extra," try *Black Medicine*, three volumes filled with lethal tricks, prepared by N. Mashiro.

Rounding off your education in the field of homicide, you should consider certain specialties. *The Terrorist Explosive Handbook* is a nifty volume, penned by Jack McPherson, that will fill you in on combat demolitions. *Crossbows*, edited by Roger Combs, provides an interesting alternative to firearms when you're plotting that assassination scene. The handling of edged weapons is covered by David Steele, in *Secrets of Modern Knife Fighting*, and by Michael Echanis, in *Knife Fighting and Throwing*. Ragnar Benson surveys lethal snares in *Mantrapping* and *The Most Dangerous Game*.

If you decide on graphic wound descriptions in your fiction, first make sure you've got your physiology together. Know the proper names for organs, bones, and arteries before you start to throw the terminology around. (I still recall an episode of "Andy Griffith" where Don Knotts, as Barney Fife, discusses ailments of the "larnyx" and "medulla oblongala.") Realism may require that you determine how fast individuals of given height and weight may bleed to death from a specific wound. Has anybody ever *really* died from being hit with such velocity that nasal cartilage was driven through the brain? Which muscles have been damaged when your hero takes a bullet in the upper thigh? The answers will be found in *Gray's Anatomy* or any comparable text. I also recommend that you consult the leading homicide investigation manuals for text (and juicy photographs) depicting the results of gunshots, stabbings, strangulation, poisoning, incineration, and assorted other forms of lethal violence.

The Weaker Sex?

Sex—and sometimes plenty of it—is the other "problem" fact of life in action novels. Touching different nerves (I hope!) than homicidal violence, sexuality in genre fiction is approached by different authors and their editors in a variety of ways. Some publishers attempt to minimize the number of encounters, keeping all the hot-and-heavy action carefully offstage, while others cling to bedroom quotas, doggedly insisting on a minimum of three or four "wet" scenes per manuscript. As previously noted, readers in the genre aren't unanimous in their reactions to the topic, either, but they come prepared to see their heroes strip for action every now and then.

Despite their relegation to subordinate positions in the "normal" action novel, women are a constant feature of the genre. They appear most commonly as damsels in distress or bedmates of selected male protagonists; assorted other "female" roles include the relatives of leading men (habitually placed in jeopardy, as variations of the damsel in distress), assorted secretaries, lab technicians, or computer operators, and assorted sexy spies who function smoothly "under cover." Female victims frequently evolve into the role of lovers after being rescued by the hero of the moment, letting body language stand as an expression of their gratitude.

So much for tried-and-true clichés. As noted previously, action novels show a rising trend toward strong, decisive, independent female characters. They stand and fight beside their men — and, sometimes, carry out a ticklish mission without the benefit of male assistance. Shrinking violets are unlikely to be banished from the genre (most especially since authors, editors, and readers are predominantly male), but there are indications that the tough new breed of female character is here to stay. Who knows? She may even be the wave of the future.

Working Under Cover(s)

The amount (and type) of sex in action novels varies widely with the taste of authors, editors, and publishers. In olden times, James Bond habitually found himself a lover — sometimes several — in the midst of every case, and thereby set the tone for his successors. In his debut novel, *War Against the Mafia*, Mack Bolan beds three women, but his luck is fragile. In the course of thirty-seven episodes from Pinnacle, he rarely scores again, and never in a graphic scene. Protagonists in other action series run a gamut from the likes of J. C. Stonewall, drooling over anything in skirts, to loyal, one-woman men like Edward X. Delaney.

Technical descriptions of The Act in genre fiction vary with the authors and the dramatic characters involved. While nothing is taboo, per se, an editor may limit your depiction of a graphic scene if it appears gratuitous, excessive, or inevitably destined to offend your audience. (Few novels focus on the graphic sexual abuse of children, for example, and your heroes probably should not display a fondness for the sadomasochistic joys of bondage.) Based on a perusal of the literature, it is apparent that your sex scenes need not be hard-core to be effective.

Notice how suggestive dialogue can sometimes serve in place of sweaty thrusting, as when Dean Koontz gives his characters a break in *Twilight Eyes*:

> *Rya pulled off her sopping tennis shoes and socks, then skinned out of her wet T-shirt. Beads of water glimmered and trembled on her bare arms, shoulders, breasts.*

"You could have been killed," I said.

She slipped off her shorts and panties, took another sip of brandy, came to me.

"Were you hoping to get killed, for Christ's sake?"

"Hush," she repeated.

I was shuddering uncontrollably.

She seemed calm. If she had been afraid during the climb, the fear had left her the moment she touched ground again.

"What is it with you?" I asked.

Instead of answering, she began to undress me.

"Not now," I said. "This isn't the time—"

"It's the perfect time," she insisted.

"I'm not in the mood—"

"Perfect mood."

"I can't—"

"You can."

"No."

"Yes."

"No."

"See?"

In *Child of Blood*, I used a similar technique and let my readers fill the gaps with their imaginations:

She set the brush aside and considered her reflection in the mirror. "Two gray hairs this week. That proves it."

Kneeling at her side, he slid an arm around her waist. "I've got a thing for older women."

"Pervert." But she had to catch her breath as he nibbled on her earlobe, nuzzling the soft curve of her neck. "That's nice."

He slipped his hand inside her robe and cupped one pliant breast, the nipple coming to attention in his palm. He teased it with his thumb and felt her shiver at his touch.

"You're not so old."

"I'm feeling younger all the time."

His hand slid between her thighs until she clamped her legs around his wrist and held it captive.

"Now I've got you."

"Not a chance. The hand is quicker than the eye."

"You'll have to prove it, mister. Oh . . . oh, yes . . . right there."
He brought her to the edge, then drew his hand away. "Where are you going?"

"Bed. We old folks need our sleep."

"Too late." She followed him, her robe forgotten on the chair.

Good taste aside, the timing of a sex scene should be logical, appropriate to the progression of your story. Characters may not have time (or energy) for making love within the context of a tale that spans a single day or less, with hectic chases, shootouts, and the like to keep them hopping. Even macho men get tired, sometimes, and flying lead can have disastrous effects on the libido.

Still, a sex scene *may* fit in at unexpected junctures of a story, if you have established opportunity and motive. Desperation in the face of almost-certain death is frequently employed as an excuse for characters to grab a quickie for the road. Besieged by nameless horrors in a rural supermarket, two of Stephen King's protagonists reach out for one another in "The Mist":

We went up the narrow flight of stairs and into the office. It was empty, as she had said. And there was a lock on the door. I turned it. In the darkness she was nothing but a shape. I put my arms out, touched her, and pulled her to me. She was trembling. We went down on the floor, first kneeling, kissing, and I cupped one firm breast and could feel the quick thudding of her heart through her sweatshirt. I thought of Steffy telling Billy not to touch the live wires. I thought of the bruise that had been on her hip when she took off the brown dress on our wedding night. I thought of the first time I had seen her, biking across the mall of the University of Maine at Orono, me bound for one of Vincent Hartgen's classes with my portfolio under my arm. And my erection was enormous..

We lay down then, and she said, "Love me, David. Make me warm." When she came, she dug into my back with her nails and called me by a name that wasn't mine. I didn't mind. It made us about even.

In *Prairie Fire* (Gold Eagle, 1984), the Executioner is cornered on a small midwestern farm, surrounded by his enemies, when he enjoys an unexpected close encounter with the lady of the house:

> *"Toni, listen—"*
>
> *"No," she told him flatly, interrupting. "You said it yourself; this is all the time we have. Tonight we may . . . ." She hesitated, swallowed hard around the knot of fear and tension in her throat, and tried again. "I don't intend to waste my last few hours by denying what I feel."*
>
> *He looked at her and understood the yearning that so often gripped combatants on the eve of mortal conflict. Something in the human animal demanded it, an affirmation of survival in the face of violent death.*
>
> *And was there more to it than that? The soldier neither knew nor cared. He shared the lady's urge, her primal passion.*
>
> *"They're expecting us inside," he said, and knew before he finished speaking that it sounded lame.*
>
> *"So they are."*

As in the realm of violence, pitfalls wait here for careless writers. Brainless bimbos who immediately spread their legs for any man who buys a round of drinks or offers them a compliment are hopelessly cliché. Some such exist, of course, but when your hero has his way with every woman he encounters, you are veering out of genre fiction into adolescent fantasy. Likewise, if you discover that your female characters are frequently excited by the thought of violent rape, you need to think again. This caveman attitude is totally passé, and anyone who doesn't recognize the fact is sadly out of touch with modern-day society.

Your characters should keep the facts of life in mind as they pursue their various adventures. Contraception may be something to consider, and your people should be normally aware of AIDS, venereal disease, and so on. I am not suggesting that your novel should become a condom advertisement, but your hero may look foolish, in this modern day and age, if he engages frequently in random couplings with total strangers. (The odds are stacked against him as it is, remember, what with terrorists and mafiosi breathing down his neck. Unless it fits your story line, he doesn't need disease to make things worse.)

Your choice of genre grants you ample opportunity to probe the boundaries of good taste, but there is something to be said for self-restraint. A violent confrontation can be artfully described and still deliver where it counts, without a quart of blood or heap of brains thrown in for emphasis. You can deliver an erotic scene without examining each orifice in microscopic detail or resorting to the tired clichés of pulp pornography. As any feminist can tell you, gross, exaggerated sex scenes usually have their roots in twisted views of women.

(Perhaps the oldest, most offensive sexual cliché revolves around the female character who loses self-control in public places, at the least appropriate of times. In *Jakarta Coup*, a female executioner—and communist, of course—is so excited by the act of shooting helpless victims that she lifts her skirt and starts to stroke herself. An equally repugnant scene, depicted in *Behind the Door*, finds "heroine" Elizabeth Shea "betrayed by her body," growing hopelessly aroused at the sight of a friend being raped by two hospital orderlies. Instead of seeking help, she starts to masturbate ferociously, in a repulsive sequence that should grab the 1988 Bad Taste Award hands-down.)

Sadistic sex and violence may be useful to a novel—normally in scenes depicting the activity or thoughts of an unbalanced villain—but you should beware of making them the *reason* for your story. And remember, please, when dealing with the rough stuff, that a little goes a long, long way.

Your characters are not expected to lead hum-drum "normal" lives; far from it. But they are not Supermen and women, either. Bear in mind that they are human beings, vulnerable to the injuries, diseases, and emotional assaults that plague their peers. You *can* invest your people with a measure of humanity without creating nerds and weaklings. In the long run, I suspect your readers may be grateful for the change of pace.

10. "It Seemed So Real!"

Homework time. Again.

I've said it more than once, and I assert the author's right to repetition here. To make it in the action field, your work must be (or *seem*) authentic. Sure, I know you're writing fiction, but that simply means your characters and plot are fictional. It doesn't mean you dream up all the technical material to suit your fantasies as you proceed.

I cannot overemphasize the fact that many of your readers will have backgrounds in the military, law enforcement, or intelligence. It may not make them geniuses, per se, but I can guarantee it doesn't make them dummies, either. Each of them is thoroughly conversant with the hardware and the operational procedures in their field of expertise, and they can spot a phony in an instant. Never mind the fact that they are reading action novels to escape from day-to-day reality. They're after the adventure, granted, but they want it couched in realistic terms, with weapons, vehicles, and other pieces of equipment that perform correctly in a world where all the laws of nature still apply.

Of course, having a background in the military or intelligence, police work, or any technical or scientific field may assist you in your writing. We've discussed the benefits of "writing what you know," but don't despair if your experience does not include a stint of military service, graduate degrees in astrophysics, or the like. It isn't necessary to assassinate a man before you write a murder story, and your readers should be willing to accept a ringer, *if you do your homework*.

Stories may arise from many sources. *Red Storm Rising*, a phenomenal best-seller for Tom Clancy, grew out of the author's interest in a board game. It's a long way from the writer's den to World War III, but Clancy made the leap in style — and so can you, if you apply yourself. The key, for those of us who don't possess encyclopedic knowledge of the world at large, is *research*.

Sound familiar? I should hope so. We've already looked at sources of material on background for your characters (in Chapter 7), on languages and jargon (Chapter 8), and on weapons and their handling (Chapter 9). Please don't be intimidated when I say that we have barely scratched the surface of our research. Bear in mind that *you* picked out a story line and sketched a plot because it sounded interesting to *you*. It shouldn't cost you much in terms of human suffering, therefore, to take some time and study up on information you may need to make the story work. If you are bored to tears while doing research on your topic, I suggest you do us all a favor and forget it. If the author has no interest in his story, why should anybody else?

Essentials

Before we tackle the specifics, I feel duty-bound to scrutinize an action writer's basic reference shelf. What's that? You thought your favorite authors simply knew it all, and poured their boundless knowledge onto paper as the stories came to life? So sorry. Guess again.

No matter how you manage to approach the action genre, you will need at least a general familiarity with world affairs and politics. Why's that, you ask? Because, dear friends, assassination, terrorism, war, and all the other juicy stuff begins with *people*, arguing — and ultimately killing — over territory, ideology, self-interest. If you're not aware of who hates whom, and why, smart money says your fiction will be seriously short on depth and understanding.

Politics and world affairs are no great mystery. Subscribe to any of the major weekly magazines — like *Newsweek*, *Time*, or *U.S. News & World Report* — to keep abreast of recent action. Daily papers and the evening news are valuable story sources, as we noted earlier, and you should add at least one major daily to your shopping list. A current almanac should certainly be added to your reference shelf, and you can glean valuable information from yearbooks issued by the publishers of various encyclopedias.

Regardless of your story's setting, foreign or domestic, you will have to grapple with geography. It's nice if you can travel widely, do your research on location, and enjoy a tax-deductible vacation in the bargain. If, however, you cannot afford a trip to Northern Ireland, Lebanon, South Africa, or Bangkok, don't give up. The necessary information is available and well within your grasp.

A good world atlas is essential to your bookshelf. Twenty dollars, give or take, will put you in the game with fairly detailed maps of every nation in the world, the fifty states, and sundry other information on the population, customs, climate, languages, and other trivia about your chosen field of operation. Tourist guidebooks can be helpful, filling in the details on hotels, historic landmarks, ethnic neighborhoods, and so forth. If your people do their hunting stateside, buy yourself a decent road atlas of the United States for openers. Street maps of specific cities are available from libraries, gas stations, tourist bureaus, chambers of commerce, or your automobile club. Incorporation of real streets and landmarks lends authenticity to your writing, but watch out for libel suits while you're at it. Use local telephone directories — available in major libraries — to weed out names of actual establishments and individuals, sparing yourself some serious headaches. (You'd be surprised, but the proprietor of Tony's Bar and Grill on Elm Street may resent depiction of his business as a gay bar, a sleazy doper hangout, or a front for agents of the KGB.)

A final word on general sources. I enjoy the several *People's Almanacs*, prepared by David Wallechinsky and his father, novelist Irving Wallace. Certain information in the trade-size volumes has grown dated over time, but they still brim with priceless bits of obscure history, political trivia, and information on "Who *Really* Rules" various nations of the world. Another vital source, for me, has been *What's What*, a "visual glossary" of everyday objects, edited by Reginald Bragonier and David Fisher. If you've ever felt the urge to look inside a fighter airplane's cockpit, puzzled over the internal mechanism of a pistol, or simply wondered what to call the plastic tips you find on shoelaces, *What's What* is the book for you. Any time you're at a loss for words, you simply find the illustration of a uniform, a vehicle, a hairdo — name it — and the several parts will be concisely labeled, making sure you get it right the first time, every time. I cannot overemphasize the value of this single volume, which has served me well on literally every book I've written since it fell into my hands.

Okay, enough on basics. When you come to the specifics of your story, you will find (thank God!) that books and articles exist on *everything*.

Unless you've just imagined something on your own, I can assure you someone, somewhere, has described your chosen process, place, or thing in print. From A to Z, it's all been covered — or it will be, by the time you get around to plotting out your novel. There is no excuse for any modern novelist to write from ignorance and try to fake it as he plods along.

We obviously don't have time or space to mention every reference book available on every subject known to humanity. Consult your local library or scan the subject index of *Books in Print* for a sampling of sources on your chosen topic. While you're at it, don't forget the *Reader's Guide to Periodical Literature*, an annual index of magazine articles published in English, covering virtually any subject you can name.

The good news is, we *do* have time to list some special sources that may come in handy for adventure writers, whether you are doing paramilitary work, police procedurals, or techno-thrillers. Authenticity is still the key, across the board in genre fiction, and a sampling of the titles listed here should get you started.

Rolling Thunder: Use of Military Vehicles

Military vehicles and hardware play a crucial part in modern action novels, but you needn't be an engineer or jet mechanic to produce a realistic manuscript. Technology is waiting at your fingertips, and if you feel inventive — as Clive Cussler did in *Firefox* — information on existing hardware may be helpful when you sit down to design your own.

If you intend to deal with aircraft in your story, keep a weather eye on nomenclature, capabilities, and armament. The necessary information may be gleaned from works like *NATO Air Power Today*, by Michael Gething; *USAF Today*, by Dana Bell; or *US Naval and Marine Aircraft Today*, by Don Linn. Robert Jackson takes you into the cockpit with *Flying Modern Jet Fighters*, and Larry Davis conducts a combat tour in *Gunships*. Whirlybirds receive adequate treatment in Michael Gething's *Military Helicopters*, and in two volumes by Paul Beaver: *Attack Helicopters* and *Modern Military Helicopters*.

Taking your war to the sea, you will probably want to peruse *Jane's Fighting Ships*, a definitive source, which also costs the proverbial arm and a leg. More affordable volumes include Paul Beaver's *NATO Navies of the 1980s*, along with *The U.S. Navy Today* and *Soviet Navy Today*, both by Milan Vego. Subsurface action is covered by Paul Beaver, in *Nuclear-*

Powered Submarines, and in *Submarine Warfare Today and Tomorrow*, by John Moore and Richard Compton-Hall.

An army may travel on its stomach, but few leave their vehicles behind. Coverage of the subject may be found in *Modern American Armor*, by Steven Zaloga and James Loop; in *Tank War Vietnam*, by Simon Dunstan; and in *US Infantry Combat Vehicles Today*, by Steven Zaloga and Michael Green. Simon Dunstan crosses the Atlantic for a treatment of *British Combat Vehicles Today*. Zaloga and Loop visit the Middle East with *Israeli Tanks and Combat Vehicles*, backed up by S.M. Katz in *Modern Israeli Tanks and Combat Vehicles*. Helmoed-Roemer Heitman gives us a view of *The South African War Machine*. Steven Zaloga covers "enemy" hardware in *Soviet Tanks Today*, and teams up with James Loop again to present *Soviet Tanks and Combat Vehicles*.

Researching Strategy

Miscellaneous hardware and tactics are covered in a wide variety of reference works. Among the more intriguing are Duncan Long's *Modern Ballistic Armor*, dealing with "bulletproof" gear, and Peter Stiff's *Taming the Landmine*. If one of your characters is facing a polygraph examination, you may want to browse through Vlad Kalashnikov's *Beat the Box: The Insider's Guide to Outwitting the Lie Detector*. Pursuit of missing persons is covered handily in *You Can Find Anyone*, by Eugene Ferraro, and preparation of false identities is examined in *New I.D. in America*, by an anonymous author.

Accurate portrayal of military (or paramilitary) tactics is central to many action/adventure novels. If you're a veteran yourself, no problem. If you're not, relax and check out several of the references available to one and all. *Guerilla Warfare*, by Bert Levy, will provide the basics for a war of hit-and-run, while Steven Zaloga takes you *Inside the Soviet Army Today* for a look at the opposition. J. K. Cilliers provides a close-up view of African combat in *Counter-Insurgency in Rhodesia*, and John Wiseman, former SAS instructor, teaches his readers how to *Survive Safely Anywhere*. Your people have to eat while living off the land, and you will find some pointers—not to mention earthy recipes—in *The Green Beret Gourmet*, by James Guttenberg. Down-and-dirty police tactics are discussed by Steven Mattoon in his *SWAT Training and Deployment*. *Ninja 1990*, by Scott French and Lee Lapin, puts a cutting edge on modern martial arts, and

Paul Elhanan examines a different side of the action/adventure business in *Keep 'Em Alive: The Bodyguard's Trade*.

It never hurts to seek your information from the horse's mouth, and in these days of declassified information, police and military field manuals are readily available through various outlets. Some of the better ones include the *Special Forces Handbook; Special Forces Operational Techniques; U.S. Special Forces Recon Manual;* the *Ranger Handbook; Ranger Training and Operations;* the *U.S. Navy SEAL Combat Manual; Guerilla Warfare and Special Forces Ops; Border Security and Anti-Infiltration Ops; Survival, Evasion and Escape;* the *U.S. Army Special Forces Medical Handbook; Combat Survival* (published for the British SAS); the *U.S. Army Sniper Training Manual; U.S.M.C. Sniping;* the *Police Pursuit Driving Handbook;* the *South African Anti-Terrorist Operations Manual;* and the *French Foreign Legion Para Combat Manual.* All of these, and many more, are currently obtainable through mail-order, at various sporting goods outlets, and at gun stores.

If your characters aren't facing enemy troops on the battlefield, odds are they *will* be engaged in some manner of covert activity. For background on intelligence-gathering techniques, check out Tom Kneitel's *Guide to Embassy and Espionage Communications; The Complete Spy,* by Robert McGarvey and Elise Caitlin; or *American Espionage and the Soviet Target,* by Jeffrey Richelson. Peter Helms instructs us in the fine art of *Countering Industrial Espionage,* while Gregor Ferguson explains techniques for toppling hostile governments in *Coup d'Etat.*

Our list of titles barely samples the available material, but it should give you an idea of all the goodies that are out there, waiting for you to incorporate their "secrets" in your fiction. Given the variety and wealth of information at your fingertips, it seems incredible that any modern author would attempt to wing it, sprinkling the text with clumsy errors. Still, it happens.

If you keep your wits about you and devote the necessary time to background research on your subject, you can rest assured it won't be happening to *you.*

11. Breaking In

In *QB VII*, author Abraham Cady is invited to address a class of would-be Hemingways upon the subject of creative writing. "How many of you want to be writers?" he asks. Every hand in the auditorium is hopefully raised. Cady studies the expectant faces for a moment, then he drops his bomb. "Why the hell," he asks, "aren't you home *writing*?"

Gotcha. And he has a point, of course . . . but, then again, there's more to life than art and poetry. You don't believe me? Fine. Come lunchtime, slap some mustard on your latest manuscript and have a ball.

I grant you, many modern authors qualify as artists (though the best of them have difficulty with pretentious labels). Many more are adequate mechanics, tuning up their prose until it has the guts to leave a standing start and break the mark at seventy across a quarter-mile. A few of those will go the distance and aspire to art or affluence—the two are *not* synonymous—but dreams don't mean a thing unless their writing finds an audience. Picasso didn't hang *Guernica* in a closet, and you've got no business hiding all your best ideas in drawers and notebooks, either.

Here it is; we've reached the bottom line. Unless you want to live and die a "wanna-be" who never was, you have to *publish*. Not just think about it, mind you, or discuss it with your family and friends. You have to *do* it. And, despite your best intentions, your determination of the moment, *doing* it may not be quite the piece of cake that you imagine.

In my teaching days, before I managed to escape the rat race and devote myself to full-time writing, I was treated to a case in point. One of my colleagues was a more-or-less professional musician, playing nights and weekends with assorted bands around Las Vegas. On the side, he cranked out more than fifty songs, complete with music, demo tapes, the whole nine yards. He hired a printer to prepare and package his material. He registered the songs with ASCAP and applied for copyrights. From all appearances, he was prepared to make it big and kiss the school good-bye.

The rest is silence.

Why? Because my friend devoted all his time and energy to "getting ready" for success. He scoured each and every word for typos, agonized for hours over glitches in his tapes, had copies of his music printed up in several sizes, bound in handsome covers. And he never sent the damned things off to a prospective buyer.

I'm no Sigmund Freud, but I can recognize the fear of failure when I see it. Then again, I may be off the mark. It's possible my friend was frightened of *success*. No matter. Either way, it all came out the same. He sat around and talked about his work, the songs collected dust, and he was going nowhere fast. I'm betting he's arrived by now.

It's normal to be jumpy, nervous, apprehensive when your work is on display for strangers. Seasoned veterans live with fear of failure and rejection just like any first-time writer, but they *don't* allow anxiety to paralyze them in their tracks. They keep on working, and if this or that beloved project hits a snag, they've always got another waiting in the wings. I'm not convinced that cheaters never prosper, but I guarantee that *quitters* haven't got a chance.

Scoping Markets

Before you can attempt to make a sale, you have to know your market. If you've done your homework, you already know which publishers are turning out adventure novels, what their product looks like, who their leading authors are. Before you make the leap toward offering your work for sale, consult a published guide like *Literary Market Place* or *Writer's Market*. Both list publishers of books and magazines, their editorial requirements, subject matter preference, and rates of pay. (They also offer lists of literary agents, but we'll come to that in time.)

Despite the popularity of action novels—an estimated fifty series are in the stores at any given time—the field is dominated by an even dozen of the country's several thousand publishers. Appearing alphabetically, they are:

Avon Books
105 Madison Avenue
New York, NY 10016

Avon's action offerings include the *Killsquad* series; they have produced single titles such as *Glitz, Mr. Majestyk, Tales of the Wolf,* and *The Fifth Horseman*.

Ballantine Books
201 East 50th Street
New York, NY 10022

Ballantine publishes the *Chopper 1, Kane's War,* and *Private Eye* series under its Ivy imprint. Single-title offerings include *The Traveler* and *In the Heat of the Summer*.

Bantam Books
666 Fifth Avenue
New York, NY 10103

Action offerings from Bantam include the *Hatch* and *Dennison's War* series. Genre entries in the single-title field include *Child of Blood* and the various best-sellers produced by Robert Ludlum.

Berkley/Jove
200 Madison Avenue
New York, NY 10016

Adventure series from Berkley/Jove include the *M.I.A. Hunter, Deadly Force, The Guardians, The Hard Corps, The Brotherhood of War,* and *The Corps*. According to its recent listings, Berkley/Jove does not accept unsolicited manuscripts or queries. In plain language, that means you'll need an agent if you hope to break in here.

Critic's Choice Paperbacks
31 East 28th Street
New York, NY 10016

Critic's Choice is the new kid on the block in action publishing. They turn out an average of 96 titles per year, selected from an estimated 100 submissions. Those are pretty fair odds for beginners with talent, and may compensate for the company's low average advance payment

($1,000). Recent action titles include *Morning Ran Red*.

Dell Publishing Company
1 Dag Hammarskjold Plaza
New York, NY 10017

Action offerings from Dell include the *Death Merchant* and *Traveler* series. Single titles include *Crossfire* and *Centrifuge*. Dell has strict procedures for submission and does not release the names of editors. Check *Novel and Short Story Writer's Market* for specifics here, and follow their directions to the letter.

Gold Eagle Books
225 Duncan Mill Road
Don Mills, Ontario, Canada M3B 3K9

Dominating the market created by Pinnacle in the late 1960s, Gold Eagle leads the modern field with series like *Mack Bolan*, *Able Team*, *Phoenix Force*, *SOBs*, *Vietnam: Ground Zero*, and *Deathlands*. After years of concentration on series work, this publisher is now coming on strong with single titles, including *Kiev Footprint*, *China Maze*, *Nuke Hill*, *A Talk with the Angels*, and *Night of the Running Man*.

New American Library
1633 Broadway
New York, NY 10019

Under its Signet imprint, NAL produces action series such as the *Destroyer*, pioneered by Pinnacle. Hot single titles include *Year of the Dragon* and *Confessional*.

Warner Books
666 Fifth Avenue
New York, NY 10103

Switch-hitting with its Popular Library imprint, Warner turns out the *Cody's Army* and *Avenger* series. Single-title entries include *Cover*, *Scorpion*, and *Hour of the Assassins*.

Zebra Books
475 Park Avenue S.
New York, NY 10016

Running close behind Gold Eagle in the action market, Zebra shows a strong affinity for postapocalyptic fiction in series like *Endworld*, *Ashes*, *The Survivalist*, and the *Doomsday Warrior*. Vietnam fiction is represented by the *Black Eagle* and *Gunship* series. In 1988, Zebra also revived the Pinnacle imprint, beginning with reissues of the original *Executioner* novels by Don Pendleton.

Picking Out an Agent

Before we tackle the mechanics of submitting work to these (or other) publishers, a word about selection of—and the desirability of working with—a literary agent. Do you need one? Why? And, if you do, how should you choose one from the hundreds currently available?

Unfortunately, there are no pat answers. Agents have their uses, but they aren't infallible, and signing on with one is *not* a guarantee of fame and fortune. At this writing, I've sold eighty books; *two* of those were sold through an agent, and some of the others were sold from outlines and proposals he declined to handle. It's a fickle, crazy business, but the unpredictability is part of its allure . . . at least, it is for me.

Working with an agent offers some definite advantages. If you choose correctly, you will have the benefit of widespread contacts in the business, expertise with contracts, and your agent's skill at pulling down top dollar on a sale. Some publishers (and most screenplay producers) deal exclusively with agents, trashing unsolicited material without a second glance. A decent agent also offers criticism of your work, from start to finish, keeping manuscripts on track and putting mammoth egos in their proper place. (Okay, I *know* it hurts to hear your work described as less than perfect, but I'd rather take my lumps at the proposal stage, correct my various deficiencies, and grab that sale. My ego doesn't pay the rent.)

Selection of an agent isn't quite as complicated as it sounds. Obtain a list of possibles from *Literary Market Place*. Listings should include an agent's field of interest (general fiction, Westerns, mysteries—whatever), fees, and possibly the titles of some recent sales. The number of an agent's clients may be listed, and some well-known names might be thrown in for emphasis.

Some agents charge a "reading fee" for first-time, unsolicited material, but you should check out the fine print before you part with any cash. Is it a one-time-only fee? Are you entitled to a refund if your manuscript is sold? Will you be getting anything besides a simple "reading" for your money, such as helpful criticism and advice? The reading fee is perfectly legitimate, but you should stay away from agents who depend on fees instead of book sales for their daily bread and butter.

When you've settled on an agent—and the agent has agreed to work with *you*—you may be asked to sign a contract. Understand its terms before you take the plunge. Will your selected agent handle *all* your work, or only items in a certain subject area? If he or she rejects a book, will you be free to sell it on your own? And if you do secure a freelance sale, are you required to pay your agent a percentage, even though he took no part in the negotiations? Will you be "typecast" by your agent, forced to stick with mysteries or action novels when you'd like to take a fling at science fiction?

Literary agents come in every shape and size; their capabilities and ethics run the gamut of the human rainbow. Before you make a final choice, I recommend you take a look at Michael Larsen's *Literary Agents: How to Get & Work With the Right One for You.* It's cheap insurance and an education, all rolled up in one.

Close Encounters

Regardless of your final choice, an agent or the more direct approach to publication, you will have to put your grand ideas on paper and submit them for review. There are two basic schools of thought on the mechanics of submission: many authors start a book and see it through before they seek a publisher, while others try to make the sale ahead of time, with query letters, a proposal, and/or sample chapters of their work. I've tried both angles of attack, and I prefer the latter, thereby saving loads of time and keeping several projects on the fire, in case one doesn't make the cut. I don't keep stacks of dusty, unsold manuscripts around the house, because they don't exist.

Whatever your approach, a query letter should initiate submission of your work. (Do not—I say again, DO NOT—approach an editor by telephone without a personal, advance request. At best, your call will be rerouted and ignored; at worst, the editor will carry memories of what a pushy, egocentric amateur you are.) Unless a publisher specifically requests completed manuscripts, don't even *think* of sending off a finished novel. It's like picking out a total stranger on the street and asking him or her to marry you; you may not get your face slapped, but the chances are you won't be picking out a silver pattern, either.

Query letters lay the basic groundwork for submission, introducing you and your ideas to a prospective publisher. They should include a "hook," a brief synopsis of the story, and a summary of published credits for the author. If you've published many articles or books, select a few of recent vintage for your list. If you're a novice, skip the credits, and for heaven's sake don't call attention to yourself with lines like: "While I've never published anything before, I'm certain I can do a bang-up job." Experience is not essential in the writing game, but flaunting *in*experience can be the kiss of death.

I've reproduced below a query letter that I used to sell a book in early 1988. The project wasn't fiction, but the principles involved remain the same. (Names and addresses have been changed to protect the innocent.)

Mr. Amos Quigley
Editor: Bonanza Books
711 Sunset Blvd.
Los Angeles, CA 90052

Dear Mr. Quigley:

America today is caught up in the grip of what one expert calls a "homicidal mania," besieged by transient monsters, dubbed "serial" killers or "recreational" murderers, who stalk their human prey at random, killing as a grisly form of sport. According to the FBI's best estimate, the random killers in our midst assassinate 5,000 victims annually—for an average body-count of thirteen murders each and every day, year-round.

I am a professional author with 68 books published since 1977 and nine more under contract at the present time. (For a partial listing of my work, please see Contemporary Authors, Volume 108.) My latest novel, Child of Blood, is scheduled for release by Bantam Books, in May. My contributions to the "Executioner" series, from Gold Eagle, have sold more than three million copies in paperback.

I propose the publication of a new, encyclopedic volume covering case histories of some 400 serial killers identified in the 20th century. The working title for my book is <u>Hunting Humans</u>, and I will be happy to supply you with a sample of my work, on spec, at your request.

Sincerely yours,

Mike Newton

In a fiction query, you may wish to lead with your credentials (if you have some), or insert a hook that rivets reader interest in the central premise of your plot. Don't lay the story out in detail. Sales aren't made from query letters; hence, your offer of a sample done "on spec" — that's free of charge, with no commitments made on either side — to show the publisher your style. A fairly detailed outline, breaking down your story into chapters, normally accompanies samples, so intended publishers can sit in judgment on the plot. (And please remember, once you sell an outline, you are duty-bound to keep at least the major points intact. If you surprise your editors with unexpected twists, they may withhold approval — and your paycheck — while you burn the midnight oil to bring your story back on track.)

An outline's length will be determined by your story, its complexity, projected length, and so forth. Editors are flexible in that regard, but watch your step on sample chapters. If they ask for two, don't send them ten; if a prospective buyer asks for thirty pages of your work, don't send off fifty or a hundred. Likewise, sample chapters are *consecutive*, from the beginning of a story. Don't send Chapters 1 and 12 because the latter happens to contain your favorite scene. The editor is interested in seeing how your style and story flow; he doesn't want to hop around and hit the "highlights" like a moviegoer watching previews of coming attractions.

If you're working with an agent, she may ask for a *proposal*, rather than an outline of your book with sample chapters. A proposal, generally speaking, is a long synopsis of your story. *How* long? For an average paperback, a length of ten or twenty pages may suffice. If you're shooting for megabucks in hardcover, you may have to crank out sixty to a hundred pages, throwing in whole scenes and snatches of dialogue, preparing what amounts to a *Reader's Digest* condensed version of your novel. Either way, your agent and your editors will want to know the ending of the story, and they may suggest revisions in the plot from time to time. Consult your agent for specifics on the length and format of proposals prior to putting anything on paper.

Once again, unless you're famous or the editors are feeling generous, do not expect to cinch a sale with your proposal. Think of it as an extended query letter, spelling out your plot in more detail and (hopefully) arousing interest in prospective buyers. Chances are, you'll still need samples of your work to close the deal, which brings us to the nuts and bolts of putting words on paper.

Nuts and Bolts

First, the basics. Please forgive me if I treat you like a rank beginner here. I know *you* know the rules of manuscript mechanics. It's the *other* guy who needs a little help, so just bear with me for a moment, eh?

For openers, your manuscript must absolutely, positively, inescapably be *typed*. That's right, you heard me. And before we start to quibble, I assure you, earnestly, that you are not the sole exception to the universal rule. Forget about the glowing compliments you get on penmanship from day to day; the plain fact is that editors won't read a hand-scrawled manuscript. Case closed. And please don't tell me that you "just can't learn to type." That's nonsense. Every high school, business school, and junior college in the Western world has typing classes readily available. A writer who won't type is like a surgeon who's afraid of knives; either way, you're in the wrong business.

It doesn't really matter *what* you type with—manual, electric, or computer—but your ribbon should be black, your paper white and standard size. The soft pastels and screaming psychedelic shades are great for letters to your friends, but they are simply not professional. Your editors don't need the thrill, and they will certainly not thank you for the headaches caused by eye strain.

Every manuscript should have a title page, including the author's name, address, and telephone number, as shown on the next page.

If you're working with a pseudonym, you type it on the title page, but *also* indicate your real name in the upper left-hand corner. Don't concern yourself with notices of copyright at this point. Reputable publishers—like

```
John Doe
P.O. Box 333
Los Angeles, CA 90004
(555) 777-1111




              BOZO'S GREAT ADVENTURE


                       by


                   Eric Studly
```

those in *Writer's Market* — aren't about to run the risk of litigation for the sake of ripping off your novel. Royalty payments are "misplaced" from time to time, and certain publishers rely too much upon the shopworn promise that "your check is in the mail," but outright theft of manuscripts is simply not a problem in the industry today.

Starting with the first page of your story, number pages clearly and consecutively, with your last name typed beside the number. Normally, we number pages at the *top*, in either right-or left-hand corners. The addition of your name—and possibly the title of your manuscript—prevents confusion if the pages should be somehow separated by an editor. Remember that the pages of your manuscript should not be stapled, taped, or bound in any way. Forget about the nifty folders that are used for college research papers. Try a simple paper clip or not, as you prefer, but *nothing else*.

A chapter heading should be centered, midway down the page. From that point on, your typing must be double-spaced, with ample margins all around. (By double-spaced, I mean two spaces vertically. Do *not* put double spaces after every word!) It goes without saying—or should—that you type on only one side of a page. What's that? You heard that Stephen King typed part of *'Salem's Lot* out on the back of milk receipts, in single-space? *So what*? The President can park all day in loading zones and get away without a ticket, too, but you are ill-advised to follow his example. Make a million bucks or so and earn yourself a name before you get creative with the rules.

I won't address myself to style, per se, but literacy and familiarity with proper English are essential to the presentation of your manuscript. It doesn't matter if you've always had a mental block for spelling. Buy the biggest dictionary you can find and look up every word you write, if necessary. Scattered typos are forgiven in the heat of combat, but habitual misspellings in a "finished" manuscript are simply inexcusable. The same holds true for sentence fragments, run-on sentences, mistakes in subject-verb agreement, punctuation errors, and assorted other careless blunders. If you have an inkling that your high school English lessons didn't take, acquire a textbook and review the basics *now*, before you find yourself embarrassed.

Each submission to an editor or agent needs a *cover letter*, briefly summing up the contents of your latest package. If you feel it necessary, slip in a polite reminder that the samples were requested back on such-and-such a date. Remember that your correspondent may be dealing with a dozen (or a hundred) writers at the moment, and your month-old query letter may not be the first thing on his mind. A brief refresher couldn't hurt—and it could save your work from accidental relegation to the slush pile.

Mail-wise, you should always send material first-class, in envelopes of proper size and shape. *Do not fold manuscripts!* If you cannot afford a postal scale, have manuscripts weighed and metered at the nearest post office. Nothing blows your first impression like a sample that arrives with postage due.

Each query letter should include a self-addressed, stamped envelope for the convenience of potential correspondents. Many editors won't answer, otherwise, so be a sport and buy the extra stamp. Submissions, likewise, should include sufficient first-class postage for return in the event of a rejection. If you don't want samples back, your cover letter should explain as much, and spare your editor the guesswork.

Publishers consider work at different speeds, depending on a sample's length, their current work load, and a host of other factors. Holidays may intervene, vacations roll around, and readers call in sick. The listings for assorted publishers in *Writer's Market* offer estimates of their response time, but the operative word is *estimates*. If Spiffy Books reports on manuscripts "within two months," you may expect the *actual* response time to be somewhat longer. Give them twice the average time, and slip a gentle query in the mail if there has still been no response. Forgo the histrionics, threats, and accusations. Never pout on paper. You're supposed to be a pro, and pros don't pride themselves on making enemies. (With ever-shifting personnel, your nemesis from Spiffy Books may wind up running Doubleday or Random House a year from now, and you can bet that he'll remember everyone who's hassled him along the way.) Assuming that your follow-up's ignored, dispatch a final letter—certified, with a return receipt—withdrawing your material. Retain a copy of the letter for your files, along with the receipt, and try another publisher.

"We're Sorry, but Your Story Doesn't Meet Our Present Needs"

Rejection comes to every author in his turn, and you should be prepared to take bad news in stride. Most publishers employ form letters to dispose of unsolicited material. Do not expect critiques with your rejection slips. The average line refers to manuscripts that "do not meet our needs [or fit our schedule] at the present time." You never *really* know if anybody's read your work or not, but either way, you've been turned down. Accept it, and move on.

Remember, first and foremost, that rejection speaks to your material and not to *you*. Despite their fabled egos, working writers don't survive for long if they insist on treating each rejection as a personal affront. The industry is rife with horror stories based on angry phone calls, death threats, post cards scrawled in blood, but writers who develop reputations for irrational behavior quickly find themselves without an audience. The bad news travels fast, believe me, and there's simply too much competition in the marketplace for editors to waste their time on lunatics.

(A common gripe concerns the use of third- or fourth-class postage to return a manuscript, when first-class postage was provided by the author. Angry writers bitch and moan about their "loss," suspecting dark conspiracies, and what's the point? Okay, I grant you Spiffy Books may owe you fifty cents, but let's get real. We're not exactly talking life-and-death here. Shine it on, and clear the mental decks for something more worthwhile — like writing.)

Don't become discouraged by rejection. Polish up your manuscript as best you can, and turn your mind to other projects while it makes the rounds. If someone offers helpful criticism in the meantime, listen carefully and try to put your pride on hold. (Remember, there's at least an outside chance they may be right!) Don't even *think* about self-publishing in genre fiction. Competition over shelf space is intense, and you will never place a book without assistance from a publisher who has his own distributors. An action writer needs his head examined if he tries to do the job himself.

Blood and Money, or the Business Side of Art

Successful authors may be artists, but they're also businesspeople who depend on writing for their daily bread and butter. Literary agents, lawyers, and accountants handle many of the working details, but a conscientious pro will take some time to learn the ropes. You may not *have* an agent, lawyer, or accountant, meaning that you'll have to take the burden on yourself. It's no great challenge, and it can be fascinating, if you know your job before you start.

The most important part of any business is the money. Publishers traditionally offer an advance against prospective royalties, meaning that you get some cash up front, deducted from your earnings later, once your book has gone on sale. (Example: If your publisher advances you $2,000 against royalties of six percent on a book retailing for $3.95, you must sell 8,333 books before you pay off the advance and start earning royalties.) Some contracts call for refunds of advances if a book does not break even, meaning that you may be forced to ante up some cash a year or two downstream. Whenever possible, hold out for nonrefundable advances when negotiating contracts with a publisher.

If you break in with series work, you may be dealing with a "work-for-hire" agreement. Basically, this makes you an employee of the publisher, without a vested interest in the series or its characters, which are created, owned, and packaged by the publishers. The pay on work-for-hire agreements varies widely, some including royalties, but you definitely won't be given public credit for your work (and may be forced, by contract, to maintain a masquerade of confidentiality). You will not share in any sale of movie, television, or dramatic rights, and any royalties provided in your contract may be limited to predetermined sums.

Keep records of your income and expenses for the tax man. Bear in mind that writers, for the most part, are considered to be self-employed; familiarize yourself with all the rules concerning estimated taxes, self-employment tax, home offices, and other regulations handled by the I.R.S. When you negotiate a contract on your own, be conscious of your rights, responsibilities, and any penalties for nonperformance binding either side. It would require another book to cover all the fine points of the business. Fortunately, several are available. I recommend the following: Leonard duBoff's *The Law (in Plain English) for Writers*; Richard Balkin's *How to Understand and Negotiate a Book Contract or Magazine Agreement*; and Bruce Henderson's *How to Bulletproof Your Manuscript*.

With practice and some preparation, you should have the business side of writing well in hand. Be cautious, use your common sense, and understand all documents before you sign. Remember that a careless businessman who loses money on a deal has no one he can blame except himself.

12. The Payoff

We've come full circle now, from sorting out ideas and shaping plots to putting them on paper, sending them away for editorial review. There's nothing you can do to speed things up, once you've delivered samples to the postman, and I recommend you have another project waiting in the wings to occupy your mind. Above all else, you must learn patience, realizing that you've reached the stage where you begin to pay your dues.

Your goal, from this point on, is getting published. Writing, as a business, has a lot in common with those advertisements in the daily classifieds: experience may not be crucial, but it's certainly preferred. Accumulating "credits" is your first priority, and at the risk of sounding crass, I will suggest you take them as they come.

A friend of mine, with more than fifty books behind him, used to spice his early queries with a mention of the fact that he had written frequently for major periodicals. He didn't mention that his "published work" consisted of assorted letters to the editorial department of his local paper . . . and the buyers never asked. The plain fact is that editors are more inclined to read your work if someone else has had the faith to publish you before.

Times change, and each new round of authors have to prove themselves in different ways. For thirty years or so, until the latter 1950s, break-ins through the pulps were all the rage. The 1960s saw a shift toward paperback pornography, and many of our leading genre authors cut their literary teeth on kinky sex. Today—good news!—your odds of breaking in with more "legitimate" material have been improved by a resurgence in the fields of action, Westerns, mystery, and horror.

Breaking in means starting at the bottom, income-wise and every other way. You won't be pulling down six figures in advance, your books won't be promoted in the same way Stephen King's are laid before the public, and the chances are you won't be autographing copies of the *New York Times* best-seller list until you've been around the track and learned the business inside out. When you can tell a story in your sleep and have the readers coming back for more, you'll know that you've arrived—and I suspect your editors will know it, too.

In short, there's really no such thing as "overnight success," in this or any other business. Sure, I've heard the stories: Mr. X from Middletown pecks out a novel, working nights and weekends, while he labors nine-to-five at some depressing, dead-end job, and *presto*! Instant millionaire. Before he has a chance to change his socks, he's sitting on the Johnny Carson show and hawking movie rights to books he hasn't even written yet.

Okay, it happens. And they still discover movie stars behind the register at K-Mart, but for every documented miracle there are a thousand ordinary people working overtime to learn their trade. In practice, writers have to build their reputations brick by brick, like everybody else. The only real exceptions seem to come with famous names attached, like Margaret Truman, Thomas Tryon, Gary Hart, and William Buckley. Not that all of the above aren't fine, proficient authors—but it's safe to say the selling power of their names was instrumental in acceptance and promotion of their novels, first time out.

Before he touched a nerve (and tapped a gold mine) with the Executioner, Don Pendleton had turned out paperbacks like *The Olympians*, *Revolt*, *The Guns of Terra Ten*, and *The Truth About Sex*. Today, with Big Mack Bolan more or less behind him, Don is going strong with characters like Ashton Ford, from Warner Books, and he has recently broken into hardcover mysteries, with the Joe Copp series.

Ken Follett, currently a wealthy brand-name author, paid his dues for years with titles like *The Shakeout*, *The Big Needle*, *Bear Raid*, and *The Secret of Kellerman's Studio*, before cracking the big time with *Eye of the Needle* and other best-sellers. Many of his older works have lately been reissued, advertised as "early Follett capers," based upon the sure-fire selling power of his name. One hand does wash the other, after all. Without the early novels, chances are that Follett never would have struck it rich. Today, his recent works bestow new life upon the old.

Martin Cruz Smith took the world of popular fiction by storm with

Nightwing, following up with the best-sellers *Gorky Park* and *Stallion Gate* a few years later. Overnight success? Not quite. Before he penned his gruesome tale of vampires vs. Navahos, Smith had compiled a long track record with titles like *Gypsy in Amber*, *The Indians Won*, *Nuplex Red*, and *The Midas Coffin*. Don't feel too embarrassed if you missed them; most were published under pseudonyms and sank without a major ripple in the marketplace.

Consider Stephen King. Another "overnight success," with *Carrie*, King had actually been writing more or less nonstop for twenty years, racking up his first sale seven years before the grim biography of Carrie White transformed his name into a household word. It was a near thing, even so: Disgusted by rejection slips, King had consigned his breakthrough novel to the trash can, but his wife retrieved it and insisted that he finish. Modern horror has never been the same.

My own experience is similar, albeit more subdued. I spent a decade writing fifty-seven books—nonfiction, Westerns, mysteries, and action yarns—before I could afford to dump a dead-end teaching job and write full-time. There were occasions when I wondered if The Break would ever come, but paying dues can have its own rewards. The opportunity to live your fantasies on paper. Paychecks, when they finally arrive. The lift you feel (come on, admit it!) every time you see your name in print.

It should not be supposed that the pursuit of "credits" justifies an author in producing trash disguised as fiction. Granted, there will always be assorted hacks around the fringes of the industry, existing hand to mouth, but none of them deserve to prosper, and the vast majority will never rise above their roots, habitually grinding out the kind of manuscripts that give genre fiction a bad name. If you aspire to hackdom, I apologize for taking up your time. If you intend to make your work the best that it can be, you need to brace yourself. There will be work involved.

Make no mistake, the full-time writer's life can be a very pleasant one. Your hours are your own—at least, they are until a deadline rears its ugly head—and you can pace yourself without a supervisor breathing down your neck and scowling when you want to break for coffee. If you feel the urge to "get away," there won't be anybody standing by the time clock with a pink slip in his hand. Your lifestyle, in comparison with others stuck in nine-to-five routines, may offer a unique amount of freedom, room to ramble, time and space to let your secret fantasies unwind.

Let's play the flip side now. Successful writing means control, self-discipline, and concentration. If you know a manuscript is due next Tuesday, you may have to skip that family barbecue or skiing trip and stick to business. Practice gets you started in the writing game, but perseverance keeps you going. Every writer must eventually find a system that facilitates the work at hand, permitting growth, encouraging experiments, while meeting deadlines all the same. In case you miss the point, I'll spell it out: No finished manuscripts, no paychecks, and you're back behind the register at Safeway, putting on a plastic grin for all those shoppers.

It's easy for imagination to explode, and would-be writers are especially prone to Walter Mittyitis. I've seen people quit their steady jobs because they sold a single story and decided they were bound for Easy Street. A writer of my personal acquaintance once invested $16,000 in a new computer on the *promise* of impressive royalties somewhere down the line. (The promisor was canned by his superiors within the year; the royalties are still at large.) Before you start to get all starry-eyed and jettison your life for something new and flashy, make damned sure you know precisely what you're doing. It can be a long walk back, with all your bridges burned.

So much for doom and gloom. The good news is that writers with intelligence, imagination, basic skills, and the determination to succeed are perfect candidates for breaking in through action and adventure markets. Whether you intend to use the genre for a launching pad (like Follett, Smith, and others) or make action writing your career, you're in the right place, at the right time.

The rest is up to you. Go on and give 'em hell.

Index

Other Books of Interest

Annual Market Books

Artist's Market, edited by Susan Conner $18.95
Children's Writer's & Illustrator's Market, edited by Connie Eidenier (paper) $14.95
Novel & Short Story Writer's Market, edited by Laurie Henry (paper) $17.95
Photographer's Market, edited by Connie Eidenier $19.95
Poet's Market, by Judson Jerome $17.95
Songwriter's Market, edited by Julie Whaley $17.95
Writer's Market, edited by Glenda Neff $22.95

General Writing Books

Beginning Writer's Answer Book, edited by Kirk Polking (paper) $12.95
Beyond Style: Mastering the Finer Points of Writing, by Gary Provost $15.95
Getting the Words Right: How to Revise, Edit and Rewrite, by Theodore A. Rees Cheney $15.95
How to Increase Your Word Power, by the editors of Reader's Digest $19.95
How to Write a Book Proposal, by Michael Larsen $10.95
Just Open a Vein, edited by William Brohaugh $15.95
Knowing Where to Look: The Ultimate Guide to Research, by Lois Horowitz (paper) $15.95
Make Every Word Count, by Gary Provost (paper) $9.95
Pinckert's Practical Grammar, by Robert C. Pinckert $14.95
12 Keys to Writing Books that Sell, by Kathleen Krull (paper) $12.95
The 29 Most Common Writing Mistakes & How to Avoid Them, by Judy Delton $9.95
Word Processing Secrets for Writers, by Michael A. Banks & Ansen Dibell (paper) $14.95
Writer's Block & How to Use It, by Victoria Nelson $14.95
The Writer's Digest Guide to Manuscript Formats, by Buchman & Groves $16.95
Writer's Encyclopedia, edited by Kirk Polking (paper) $16.95

Nonfiction Writing

Basic Magazine Writing, by Barbara Kevles $16.95
How to Sell Every Magazine Article You Write, by Lisa Collier Cool (paper) $11.95
The Writer's Digest Handbook of Magazine Article Writing, edited by Jean M. Fredette $15.95
Writing Creative Nonfiction, by Theodore A. Rees Cheney $15.95
Writing Nonfiction that Sells, by Samm Sinclair Baker $14.95

Fiction Writing

The Art & Craft of Novel Writing, by Oakley Hall $16.95
Characters & Viewpoint, by Orson Scott Card $12.95
Creating Short Fiction, by Damon Knight (paper) $8.95
Dare to Be a Great Writer: 329 Keys to Powerful Fiction, by Leonard Bishop $15.95
Dialogue, by Lewis Turco $12.95
Fiction is Folks: How to Create Unforgettable Characters, by Robert Newton Peck (paper) $8.95
Handbook of Short Story Writing: Vol. I, by Dickson and Smythe (paper) $9.95
Handbook of Short Story Writing: Vol. II, edited by Jean M. Fredette $15.95
One Great Way to Write Short Stories, by Ben Nyberg $14.95
Plot, by Ansen Dibell $12.95
Revision, by Kit Reed $13.95
Spider Spin Me a Web: Lawrence Block on Writing Fiction, by Lawrence Block $16.95
Storycrafting, by Paul Darcy Boles (paper) $10.95
Writing the Novel: From Plot to Print, by Lawrence Block (paper) $9.95

Special Interest Writing Books

The Children's Picture Book: How to Write It, How to Sell It, by Ellen E.M. Roberts (paper) $15.95
Comedy Writing Secrets, by Melvin Helitzer $16.95
The Complete Book of Scriptwriting, by J. Michael Straczynski (paper) $10.95
The Craft of Lyric Writing, by Sheila Davis $18.95

Editing Your Newsletter, by Mark Beach (paper) $18.50

Families Writing, by Peter Stillman (paper) $15.95

Guide to Greeting Card Writing, edited by Larry Sandman (paper) $9.95

How to Write a Play, by Raymond Hull (paper) $10.95

How to Write & Sell A Column, by Raskin & Males $10.95

How to Write and Sell Your Personal Experiences, by Lois Duncan (paper) $9.95

How to Write Romances, by Phyllis Taylor Pianka $13.95

How to Write Tales of Horror, Fantasy & Science Fiction, edited by J.N. Williamson $15.95

How to Write the Story of Your Life, by Frank P. Thomas $14.95

How to Write Western Novels, by Matt Braun $13.95

Mystery Writer's Handbook, by The Mystery Writers of America (paper) $10.95

The Poet's Handbook, by Judson Jerome (paper) $9.95

Successful Lyric Writing (workbook), by Sheila Davis (paper) $16.95

Successful Scriptwriting, by Jurgen Wolff & Kerry Cox $18.95

Travel Writer's Handbook, by Louise Zobel (paper) $11.95

TV Scriptwriter's Handbook, by Alfred Brenner (paper) $10.95

Writing for Children & Teenagers, 3rd Edition, by Lee Wyndham & Arnold Madison (paper) $12.95

Writing Short Stories for Young People, by George Edward Stanley $15.95

Writing the Modern Mystery, by Barbara Norville $15.95

Writing to Inspire, edited by William Gentz (paper) $14.95

The Writing Business

A Beginner's Guide to Getting Published, edited by Kirk Polking $11.95

The Complete Guide to Self-Publishing, by Tom & Marilyn Ross (paper) $16.95

How to Sell & Re-Sell Your Writing, by Duane Newcomb $11.95

How to Write Irresistible Query Letters, by Lisa Collier Cool $11.95

How to Write with a Collaborator, by Hal Bennett with Michael Larsen $11.95

How You Can Make $25,000 a Year Writing (No Matter Where You Live), by Nancy Edmonds Hanson $15.95

Literary Agents: How to Get & Work with the Right One for You, by Michael Larsen $9.95

Professional Etiquette for Writers, by William Brohaugh $9.95

Time Management for Writers, by Ted Schwarz $10.95

To order directly from the publisher, include $2.50 postage and handling for 1 book and 50¢ for each additional book. Allow 30 days for delivery.

Writer's Digest Books
1507 Dana Avenue, Cincinnati, Ohio 45207
Credit card orders call TOLL-FREE
1-800-543-4644 (Outside Ohio)
1-800-551-0884 (Ohio only)
Prices subject to change without notice.

Write to this same address for information on *Writer's Digest* magazine, Writer's Digest Book Club, Writer's Digest School, and Writer's Digest Criticism Service.